THE KALEIDOSCOPE WOMAN

and

MOSAIC MAN

AND THE COLORS OF THEIR WORLD

Interviews conducted and compiled by

RIMA LYNN XIQUES

ISBN: 978-1-54397-698-4

INTRODUCTION

Looking through my kaleidoscope, I noticed that by moving either to the left or right of the light, I could view the same colored pieces creating different and beautiful designs and patterns. This is also true of our lives, I realized; choosing to the right or the left will create different outcomes.

The essays in *Kaleidoscope Woman and Mosaic Man* reflect the opinion that some males and females are not very different from each other. Our values and priorities are basically the same, and the encouragement to our younger self is usually uplifting.

The essays in this book are composite pictures created by a variety of people responding to the following questionnaire. I invite you to take time to complete the following questionnaire and find out what type of life design and patterns you create.

- Describe your personality and character.
- What moves the spirit or inspires you?
- Who are the people you let into your life?
- What are a few of your hobbies?
- Name a few of your favorite movies.
- Knowing what you know today, what would you tell the little boy/girl inside you?
- Complete this sentence: Love is _____.

How do you relate to and deal with your family, friends, faith, health, sex, finances, educations, politics, law, profession and work and prioritize these elements in your life?

DEDICATION

This book is dedicated to every woman and man who shares the ever-growing pursuit of happiness and comradery between the sexes. To those who are always striving to know, accept, and love each other better, may your colors shine brightly!

THE KALEIDOSCOPE WOMAN

REMEMBER HER?
she is still there …
inside you … waiting
let's go get her

CHAPTER ONE

NORMA

In Memory of the Mother of Kaleidoscope Women
Written by her firstborn
Vice-President Electronics/Pilot/Scuba Diver

THIS TOO SHALL PASS

The Kaleidoscope Woman in my life was my mother! First, I am fortunate because I was raised by a Kaleidoscope Woman, and I believe I, in turn, have raised a Kaleidoscope Woman in my daughter. My mother, born in 1932, was a Kaleidoscope Woman who, even before society coined the term "women's lib," worked for the equality of women.

My mother, Norma, was a dichotomy of sorts. She was an orphan with no close family but who held family to be the most precious of all possessions. She spent her childhood being moved from place to place as a foster child. I can't say homes, because they weren't. It's surprising Mom developed into the woman she did after being told over and over that she would amount to nothing.

Mom was an optimistic woman with a strong faith, although she didn't know it until later in her life. For some time, she thought human beings were a mutation of nature. She didn't understand where negative or hurtful behavior came from. As children, my sister, brother, and I were sent to Catechism and Sunday mass only to be asked by our priest why our mother didn't attend. Mom's answer to the question was, "It's my job to put the children in your hands and your job to put them in the right direction."

Like many parents, Mom was overprotective and loving. Because she didn't come from a stable home, she tried with all her might to create one. Her tenacity in working out problems and finding solutions was only one of her many talents. Strength and word of honor were part of her philosophy and character.

I think red was Mom's aura—the red of passion, the red of suffering, and the red of anger. She was capable of feeling so much with that enormous heart of hers. Nothing was more sacred than her children; before anyone, children came first. She passed that down to me.

Inspiration came to Mom through music. In her younger life, she played the organ and, later on, the guitar. She loved to serenade my stepfather with a number of Latin tunes that reflected her Puerto Rican roots.

Privacy was very important to my mother, perhaps because she didn't trust many people beyond her family. This also meant that she didn't have many friends as a young woman, though I do remember her friendship with Sue, one of our neighbors in the projects; Mom learned Yiddish phrases from Sue and then passed them down to me. As Mom became older, she learned to trust people a little more but still remained cautious about the intentions of most people. Although she affected people's lives positively with her friendly manner, she didn't have many close friends.

Knowledge inspired and moved this Kaleidoscope woman. Mom got her first job by getting on the wrong bus and ending up in front of Loral Electronics in the Bronx (later bought by Lockheed Martin). She started her first job there in the mailroom, and, as the story goes, she worked her way up. After first earning an associate's degree, she inquired how she could earn more money. The answer she received was, "Get yourself a bachelor's degree." And so she did. Eventually, she earned her master's degree in business, with honors, at Baruch College in Manhattan. All this while working full-time and raising three children.

I would have to guess that to her little girl within, she would say, "They were all wrong. Through love, determination, focus, and discipline you did it! You never gave up!"

Mom was a sensual woman. Though we never talked about this, you could tell by the way she moved and danced. She used to say that the woman is always the catalyst for sex. And I think she lived by that belief.

This Kaleidoscope Woman was amazing when it came to her finances. I think her instincts were developed at a very young age. As a child, she had nothing: She made her dolls out of a washcloth that she used to clean house. She would sing on the streets of Puerto Rico for pennies that she would save in a sock. When she had her three children—me being the oldest— she began putting dollars into envelopes for monthly expenses. That is where the expression "take from Peter to give to Paul" came from; she would take money from the food envelope and give it to the rent envelope. As mom's salary increased so did her desire to save money for the future. Eventually, she saved a nice amount in her IRA, stocks and bonds, and property. Thanks to Mom's vision for the future, my sister, brother, and I were able to get a little jump on our own finances.

This Kaleidoscope Woman also developed a philosophy about politics. When you're young and need help, Democrats offer all the goodies; when you're older and have earned some money, you don't want anyone to take it away. It seemed logical to me. So when I was young, I supported all the "help me" programs, but as I began earning some money, I realized I wanted to spend it and give it away in a manner that felt comfortable to me, not the government. During her older years, Mom became a staunch Republican, and some of that rubbed off on me, although I consider myself an Independent because I don't vote so much for party as for issue.

This awesome Kaleidoscope Woman was definitely born before her time. Norma was a licensed scuba diver and licensed pilot. We have photos of her smiling with a shark behind her, thirty feet below sea level. She played a mean Maj Yon, made her own jewelry, and played pinochle.

One of Mom's favorite sayings was, "This too shall pass." Now that I am older, I agree. If the situation is sad … it will pass. If the situation is happy … it will pass. Life is a constant series of change.

CHAPTER TWO

NICOLE

Instructional Designer
Learning and Development Manager

THE UNGUARDED HEART

Yes, Nicole identifies with being a Kaleidoscope Woman but doesn't feel she's a goddess or end-all/be- all. At times, she fails. She is someone who falls and learns from life and chooses to still grow in her path. She is someone who wants to really take in the different aspects of who she is—what serves her and what doesn't. And she's always willing to grow in life rather than staying stuck in place. Nicole wants to maintain and grow as a woman day by day, even in the little things; she wants to continue building all aspects of her life.

One of the Nicole's fears is being unfulfilled and remaining stagnant—just existing in the everyday norms and status quo of what society tells her, rather than living into her own vision. Negative childhood experiences have created fear of being relationally abandoned, of being alone. Although she travels quite a bit, this woman is afraid of flying, and because of the unknown, she is also afraid of death.

Purple is Nicole's favorite color. Light purple, not dark. She prefers the soft color and the whimsical feeling and feminine energy that purple also encompasses in addition to what it stands for - strength, courage, and power. That mix of dark and light.

Oh, so many things move Nicole. But at the core of her being, it's the human connection. She needs to have an honest, real, authentic type of interaction with people and make a difference in this world, to let people know that they are not alone. That they are loved and meant to be here.

Until recently, women were her comfort zone, and she didn't let many others in. Other Kaleidoscope Women were her best friends. But she has learned to let the masculine energy, the male figure, into her life. And of course, kids she loves!

She rates relationships with her family as high priority; they are definitely in her upper quadrant of her life. She is extremely close to her mom and considering the strained relationship with her father, is close despite the tension. She has learned to set boundaries and speak her voice. In spite of being raised by separated parents and the accompanying challenging family dynamics, she and her brother have a close relationship.

Because Nicole couldn't count on her social/emotional needs being met by her family, she looked to outside sources like her friends for validation and self-love. She has tons of friends, perhaps too many. She learned to find friendships that feel like home instead of being a social butterfly like she used to be. She focuses on friends that add value to her life. Since meeting her her boyfriend and developing a romantic relationship she has learned to "cut the fat" and develop friends that add to her life.

This Kaleidoscope Woman is still figuring out faith. Nicole was raised a Catholic, but her family didn't attend church or follow daily rules. She attended Catholic elementary and high schools, where she was taught the Catholic religion. What does that mean currently for her? She doesn't know yet. Nicole considers herself to be very spiritual and is connected to nature. The beach, for instance, makes her feel grounded. She views faith like a kaleidoscope with many different facets, and she is still working on it.

To Nicole, being healthy encompasses the mind, body, and soul. She believes that mental health is necessary for nourishing one's state of mind and that movement—dancing, working out, or anything that feels good to the body—is most important for good health. Sometimes you just needs rest . . . absolutely taking care of yourself.

Interestingly, this Kaleidoscope Woman has a bad relationship with her finances. People have different way of coping with issues in their life; some people overwork, and some spend money. She is working through her finances and budgets, however. She and her partner talk about their finances, which she believes is an important practice. The conversations are not always comfortable, but they are part of making her stronger. Now Nicole has a plan that can't be ignored.

Education is an important part of Nicole's life. In addition to her undergraduate work in elementary education and her master's degree in instructional design, this woman thinks both formal and self-learning is what triggers your growth as a person. Another way she worked at understanding herself and growing as a woman was attending therapy after the divorce of her parents. Her motto is to do what you love and to learn through personal development.

This woman hates politics because issues are not black or white as the political world would have one believe. It seems that politics is always asking you to pick a side, and she's never been an advocate for that. It is not one side or the other.

Nicole's present position as a manager is serving its monetary purpose. It keeps her stable in the real world and a roof over her head. She truly enjoys her empowerment classes and financial security from teaching. She wants to return to motivational speaking; having that human connection and making a positive difference in the world makes her feel alive.

Hello, fellow Kaleidoscope Women. Explore and never stop believing or discovering new facets of life. Coast, but not so long that you don't move to the next level.

Nicole has recently experienced love in its genuine form by living with her boyfriend of two and a half years. Imagine, now at thirty-six she has learned that "love is always about bettering the union."

To the little girl within her, Nicole says very emotionally, "Remember, it gets easier as you grow. In your younger years, it is a struggle to find out who you are. Listen to the voice that should be heard and remind yourself that you are someone with unique traits and personality. You bring to the world something unique. Add to the colors of the world, and don't dim your light for anyone! Just shine!"

CHAPTER THREE

ANNIE

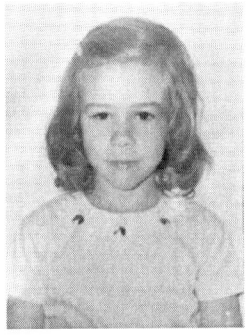

Military Admissions Advisor

A PURPOSEFUL LIFE

Does Annie identify with the Kaleidoscope Woman? Yes! She's done so many things in her life: going back to work, getting married, and having kids. After having children she decided to go back to work but found she didn't have the college background for most jobs. She was fortunate to meet the right people who offered the right opportunity at that time. It was when she moved from Venezuela and couldn't find work that her sister and sister-in-law, who were working at Merrill Lynch at the time, helped her get an interview with Human Resources, which turned into a job as a receptionist with the company.

This Kaleidoscope Woman is laid-back, but when she speaks her mind, she is heart! She voices her opinion nowadays. She is caring, likes to help others, and is a loyal person who deserves respect. Unfortunately, not everyone gains her respect.

Annie's aura is blue and green. Blue represents the tranquility of the spirit, and green is the "go get her!" color.

Beautiful sunsets and the house she is building in Tennessee are what move and inspire this woman. She loves to listen to the sounds of nature where there is no bustling city noise to obstruct her thoughts. She also loves listening to the sound of waves.

It is difficult to become a part of this woman's inner life. She wears an outer shield that is very hard for her to take off. She doesn't like being judged, because, she says, we are all different—different thoughts and backgrounds, one not better than the other. We are all the same under one God.

The number one priority in this Kaleidoscope Woman's life is family. Her family is composed of interesting characters. Sometimes they don't get along, but family always comes first and everything else is secondary.

Annie considers herself a loner, so she has a limited number of friends, and she doesn't reach out and arrange to see them that often. Other priorities like family, husband, kids and grandkids, and work are in the forefront of her life, not the other stuff.

Faith is important to Annie, but she is not a devoted Catholic and doesn't go to church. She does pray to God on her own terms—all under one God. She believes that Catholic and Jew pray to the same God—our higher power—regardless of chosen religion.

Now that this Kaleidoscope Woman is older, she thinks more about taking care of her health. In her twenties, thirties, and forties, she didn't so much. Now she checks her health with regular mammograms, pap smears, and annuals. She believes men and women should have healthcare. Other countries have systems that cover both men and women; why doesn't our country?

Right now, sex is not a priority for Annie. Of course, in a relationship it is important. Annie means that sex is important in a relationship, but sometimes medication or not enough quality time can make it hard to have a healthy sex.

Annie has an excellent relationship with money and her finances. She was taught many years ago not to owe money and not to pay interest on a credit card. If you can't afford it on a credit card, you probably don't need it, she'd say. You should pay credit-card balances at the end of the month. That's the only way to move forward. There is a big difference between what you want and what you need.

"You need to be educated to survive in this world," Annie believes. This Kaleidoscope Woman went back to school in her fifties and tells her students that if she can go back to school after thirty years, anyone can. "It's called determination."

No politics here! She doesn't like who is in power now (Trump) and doesn't want to talk about it.

As a Military Admissions Advisor, Annie likes her job but doesn't enjoy micromanaging; she's not crazy about her work environment because of the micromanaging that takes place. But she loves who she works with—the military! Since she never served time in the military, she feels it's a great honor to support and work with the active duty veterans, reserves, and spouses of our service men and women.

To her fellow Kaleidoscope Women, Annie says to take advantage of every moment in life, spread you knowledge, and educate others about what you know.

To her little girl inside, she says, "Don't regret what you do in life! Life is an experience!"

CHAPTER FOUR

MICHAEL

Retired Construction Manager

THE UNPREDICTABLE LIFE

This Mosaic Man in sensitive but not trusting of many people except his wife. He is now developing his spiritual side and trying to find out if he, in fact, has faith. Michael is a giver. He is strong, depending on the situation, and is much stronger than in his younger years. He can be headstrong and finds it difficult to forgive if someone wrongs him. It also takes him forever to forget. He considers himself to be a loner.

Blue is Michael's color of choice because it is the color of the New York Giants! This man can be moved by music, although not necessarily the lyrics. For him, inspiration comes from money and the ability to make it. He is an easy guy and goes with the flow. He is inspired by his sisters—different reasons for each.

Michael doesn't let many people into his life. He has been burned in the past and believes "Screw me once, shame on you. Screw me twice, shame on me!" He is so protective that it's hard for this man to let anyone into his life.

Family is numero uno in this man's life—not only his immediate family but also his wife's family as well. He is very close with his granddaughters. No one rules the roost except Buster, their dog. He and his wife are prince and princess. No friends by choice!

Michael shares bipolar disorder with his sister and has been on medication to remain stable. He considers himself about eighty percent healthy because of surgery that left both legs with very poor circulation. Doctors recommended pain meds for his legs but while taking them, he felt worse. As soon as he stopped the pain medication, he felt better. Extreme medications have had a terrible effect on Michael. Today he is feeling well and stable.

As a young man, Michael was very active sexually. Unfortunately, he had no respect for women and was a selfish lover. As he got older, he developed the respect and giving nature that was lacking in his younger years. He learned to please women more than himself. For the last eleven years, there has been no sex in his life. Physical age has taken a toll.

Finances take second position to family for Michael. As a kid, he learned that a person has to have money to make money. Today, he handles his finances wisely.

In spite of having an IQ of 136, Michael didn't get an advanced education. He is sorry that he never took advantage of his potential and regrets using cigarettes and drugs and making bad choices. A person survives with street smarts, and, of course, everyone needs a formal education, but the combination of both makes for a better and well-rounded life.

"Eh!" is the expression this man uses to describe his political involvement. Go with the flow is his philosophy. He has never conformed to the rules of politics. He has never voted, because he believes one vote doesn't make a difference.

Michael has worked a wide variety of jobs: hairdresser, construction, airlines, steel yard, bartender, and taxi driver. He also sang in a touring band throughout the United States.

Nowadays, this Mosaic Man is working on forgiving his mom and trying to have more faith in God. He considers himself to be very spiritual but not religious and believes that God is watching over everyone.

Michael is a man of many components. A few of Michael's phobias/fears include claustrophobia, a fear of heights, being alone, and encountering snakes, roaches, or sharks. Like a number of men he enjoys watching football; especially the New York Giants. He loves the contact and strategy of the sport. In his younger years, he played semi-pro ball and flag and touch football. He also plays guitar as a hobby.

A few of his favorite movies are *Purple Rain, Bohemian Rhapsody, Captain America*, and *Winter Soldier*.

Michael believes that A WOMAN IS priceless!

To the little boy within, he says, "Stick to your guns and use your head more instead of following your feelings. Incorporate your brains."

J E A N E T T E

Psychotherapist

THE ROAD TO CLARITY

Jeanette admires her fellow Kaleidoscope Woman, Linda. She admires her patience, her common sense, her business sense, and her calmness in the middle of a storm. She is charismatic and magnetic, and other people see these qualities in her also.

Jeanette is an intriguing, beautiful, independent, intelligent Kaleidoscope Woman with a bit of confusion that sometimes gets her in trouble. Her mental OCD (obsessive-compulsive disorder) qualities don't allow her to let go of things—positive or negative. OCD thinking can also be the source of her success. When something bothers her, she can't let it go, which can be annoying. She is a strong woman able to deal with difficult or challenging situations.

A friend invited Jeanette to President Trump's inauguration because she knew that if any problem arose, Jeanette would keep her head and not get hysterical if anything bad happened.

Jeanette's cousin from France believes she is a great business-woman. While in her late forties, and later in life, Jeanette really loved business.

Purple is the aura of this Kaleidoscope Woman—a grape color that is a combination of depth and spirituality. It also reflects a calm being often confirmed by psychics .

Jeanette is moved by beautiful music—an aria from an opera to feel connected or the human voice singing something incredible. Intelligence and speaking intelligently inspires this woman.

The people in Jeanette's life are usually present out of convenience and are acquaintances and casual friends. She will let into her life people who have the courage to analyze their own sufferings without fear. She finds she can trust such people because they look at their own suffering as an integral part of life, and they don't overreact to their own suffering. They have compassion, though the word compassion is sometimes overused.

Part of this woman believes we need to know each other better. Being similar to someone does not bring about intimacy. We can have a lot in common with someone but not be close.

"It is what it is" is the phrase that excites Jeanette about being Jeanette. She understands life as an individual journey; by living a full life and doing diverse things, one creates a unique identity. Jeanette doesn't find herself to be exciting in any specific way but feels accomplished to a certain degree. "That and a metro card will get you on the subway."

Jeanette's parents are deceased and she misses them. She is close with her brother and nephew but has had a heartbreaking experience with her daughter and doesn't wish to elaborate.

Faith fits into Jeanette's strong spiritual side. She believes we are extremely limited in understanding divinity because we are three-dimensional creatures. She thinks people who deny divinity in some shape or form are limited in their existence—like thinking the world is flat. LOVE IS beyond the obvious.

Healthwise, Jeanette is genetically lucky, and personal maintenance is something she takes care of. She concerns herself with the mental health of everyone and thinks that psychology is too often used to rationalize things away. We should remember that the cause for not every problem can be pinpointed to someone being sick or having had a terrible childhood.

This Kaleidoscope Woman is a loyal person. Once someone is in her heart, they never leave, even if they divert for a time. Interestingly enough, she felt invisible as a student in high school.

Money is essential to living, but worrying about it does not bring money to you; a positive attitude about money seems to work much better.

Education is important, but being a knowledgeable and curious person is much more important than having a formal degree. A degree is essential for certain careers, but it doesn't make you intelligent or an intellectual.

At the present time, this Kaleidoscope Woman does not relate to sex and is not sexually active. She has never been a sexually focused person. Lust was once part of her life, but it isn't anymore. She finds sex to be a complicated issue.

Politically speaking, she finds that awareness is perhaps more important than being politically active; she is more interested in the movement of power and players in the world game. She likes to know what goes on beyond what the media and public relations people try to show the public. Sometimes, she believes, the active people work with limited information; they take a stance on being politically active without the understanding and benefit of knowledge and are unaware of being manipulated. What's happening in this country is frightening her, and she feels social media has taken over.

All her opinions are based on where she is personally today. Perhaps in two years her answers will change.

To the little girl within, Jeanette says, "Being alone can bring power to you. Don't fear it!"

CHAPTER SIX

RIMA

Retired Singer, Dancer, Actress
Author

UNTIL WE MEET AGAIN

"I am woman, hear me roar," were the lyrics sung by Helen Reddy in 1972 that resonated with many, many women. There is a fire that burns in so many women, in so many ways. My fire stems from the need to create, love, and live! Since the death of my mother, Norma, in January 2018, when I found her body on the kitchen floor from a brain hemorrhage, I've heard a voice yelling at me to live!! I believe it is Mom encouraging me from heaven not to waist a bit of time on nonsense.

As I have matured, I have no patience for drama in my life. I've carefully nurtured my world of acquaintances, friends, and family to exist in relative peace and tranquility. When I was younger, I took so many things more seriously and paid an emotional price for it. Being diagnosed with Bipolar II when I was fifty years old finally helped put all the ups and downs of my life in perspective.

I feel an aura of soft, blue-purple around me that brings me peace in times of conflict. I also feel yellow at times of great happiness.

The people around me inspire much of my life and activities. My mother, sister, daughter, son, and powerful individuals inspired me to write *The Kaleidoscope Woman*, which has opened my mind and spirit to so many beautiful experiences. Unlike a few "women's libbers," I like men! I don't always understand them, but I appreciate their role in life, as I appreciate the role of every woman.

I am easily excited by the joy in people and the sound of laughter from my granddaughter. The most important relationships in my life are with my family. I have learned so much from my daughter and son, as individuals and with their partners. The ever-popular "we'll figure it out" has become a routine expression for me when looking for answers.

I have an eclectic group of friends; some friends are very supportive of me. Some friends are professional women and women who choose to remain as great leaders in the home, younger and older, married and single, gay and straight. I have been exposed to so much diversity in my professional life as a singer, dancer, and actress on the road that I find myself proud to be able to share some of my experiences with them and with you.

Take, for example, the time I was dancing in a club run by mobsters. Of course I didn't know it until I arrived. My mother always told me to act like a lady and be honest with my feelings. Well, one of the "guys," Charlie Dio (I think that was his name), asked me why a nice girl like me was dancing for a living. I was so scared that I lied and said I was dancing in order to purchase a piano. Well, thank God I never said I was dancing to buy the Brooklyn Bridge, because the following week, Mr. Dio had a baby grand piano delivered to my studio apartment on West 79th Street in Manhattan. "Wait a minute!" I stuttered, "That doesn't even fit in here. Take it back. Please take it back!" The mover said, "Charlie says the kid's got to have a piano … so here it is!"

I silently said a little prayer and thought of Mom … be honest, she would say. So I asked the movers to get Mr. Dio on the telephone (in the late 60s before cell phones). "Don't you like the color?" he asked? I told a very disappointed Mr. Dio that I was afraid of him and what I might have to do for his piano. He promised he would require nothing of me, but I finally talked my way out of keeping the piano. I did have to pay $200 for the damage that the movers did trying to wrangle the baby grand out of the apartment.

Faith is the foundation of my life. I know most people say family is their foundation, but without my faith in God, I know I would not be here; I would have checked out a long time ago. I truly believe in the spirit of Angels, because they have saved me from many situations in life and have given me beautiful visions as well. I believe in life after death. I have been regressed to many lives and truly believe that the spirit lives on. We are here to learn, and, like in school, some people are better students in life than others. God is love, and it all begins with loving yourself.

For my age, I'm told I'm healthy as an ox, whatever that means. Within the past six months, however, I have developed high cholesterol. Now, it's about everything I can't eat. That's so boring that I just watch my portions instead and eat what I like. I truly wish I had the discipline to exercise regularly and eat "properly." My children are always after me to drink more water. Ugh. I'm a coffee drinker and count on that water to make my quota of fluids.

My finances have always been a problem for me. I learned from my former husband that there are two kinds of poor people: one who learns not to be poor again and saves, and one who is poor and never learns the value of money. I am the latter. Only since Mom left us some money have I learned to budget and save for a rainy day.

I attended one semester of college, and that was a theater course at Miami Dade Community College. I have always admired people who have the discipline to attend and excel in school. But I also had an experience once that made me realize college education doesn't mean you know everything there is to know … obviously, it's an opportunity to learn. Many years ago, I worked as an executive assistant to the Vice President of Special Products at Bertlesmann Music Group. While heading to my desk one early morning, I heard a voice say, "How the fuck do you make a two-sided copy?" Needless, to say, I was shocked but came to the rescue of the VP. I took his papers and pressed the button . . . two sides. His face turned red, and I said, "You're welcome." The man made a quarter of a million dollars a year, but I was the one who knew how to make a two-sided copy. We all know what we have experienced. I believe that's pretty much the basics.

I only recently became interested in and involved with politics. That's because Mom was a very active conservative and watched Fox News 24/7. Although Fox is opinion news, it does give the other side of the left-wing news. I consider myself to be an Independent voter. I vote on the issues, not necessarily on the party. Though, like Mom, the older I get, the more fiscally conservative I become.

I can't put it more simply than . . . I love sex! As a Kaleidoscope Women, I experience it in different colors, designs, and movements. I think it's because of my creative nature that I appreciate the wonderful complexities of the experience. Now that I'm older, I enjoy it even more because I have found two amazing young friends and lovers who make the experience even more incredible. I feel beautiful, intelligent, and powerful when I am being intimate with them. They still make me feel desirable. Of course, sometimes I dare to think that I must possess something special in order to keep them coming back for more.

My message for the Kaleidoscope Woman is to remember that happiness is relative, but peace is eternal.

LOVE IS a precious luxury.

To the little girl within, Rima says, "I am proud of the woman you have become. You followed that voice, and it served you well! LIVE FREE!"

BILL

Licensed Funeral Director
Serial Entrepreneur

COLORBLIND

Bill is an extremely honest man, sometimes to a fault, prompting people to ask, "How do you really feel, Bill?" He believes in being truthful and in helping people. Life is hard, and it's important to help others and never cheat at life.

Respect, respect, and respect was his family code. Respect yourself and others. In the neighborhood where Bill grew up, a handshake was your word and reflected a good character and living the life that your desire.

This Mosaic Man has no fears or phobias.

Faith, family, friends, and forgiveness motivate Bill, though forgiveness does run against his Sicilian blood. Six o'clock was the time his family said a prayer of thanksgiving before sitting down to eat. Bill believes that one of the issues in society today is that we are breaking away from important values like family dinners. Technology is not bad, he says, if we use it to our advantage, like FaceTime. Rather than complaining about technology, we should use it as a solution. For example, one time Bill had a business meeting in Miami, which would have taken him two or three hours' drive to get to. Instead driving, he FaceTimed the client. Problem solved.

Bill looks back on his older generation with love, noting that divorce rates were lower and communication better. He has a tattoo of the sands of time.

Family and friends are both to be bolded and capitalized in Bill's world. He was very close with his grandfather and aunt. His neighborhood included Italian and Irish Catholics. After moving in the early nineties, he learned about so many nationalities and religions—Jewish and Christians and so many faiths. Goodbye, for him, is an expression that means "God be with you." Bill appreciates every breath. He meditates or takes private time for fifteen or twenty minutes a day as he thinks of his goals.

He believes in no judgment when it comes to friends. He allows everybody in his life, assuming that time will tell who people really are. Sometimes, others may need help. When meeting people, Bill will ask for their last name because it tells him a great deal about a person and also really opens them up.

On the agenda for Bill and his wife, who are an interracial couple, is starting a Foundation called Color Blind–See No Color. The mission statement begins with the letters BYE + JK + NPT, which stand for "Be Yourself Everyday" + "Judge Know One" + "Never Promise

Tomorrow." Who better to generate the goodwill and love of everyone in these challenging times?

This Mosaic Man has a vast list of interests and hobbies, which begins with football, baseball, golf, tennis, and weight training. He also enjoys water activities such as boating, jet skiing, and scuba diving. Bill has rented helicopters to ride over New York and volcanoes, and he hopes to one day become an aviator and own his own plane.

There are two questions Bill asks his children daily: 1) What did you do today that you enjoyed? 2) What did you do that you didn't like? Always look at the good first, and then you can learn from the bad.

Bill is an extremely healthy man. He exercises and goes for bi-annual checkups regularly. He takes vitamins and prefers homeopathic methods over prescription medicine if possible. Bill eats healthily, but once in a while he indulges in a special meal. Balance is the key to everything.

"Extremely important and a priority" is how this Mosaic Man describes his philosophy about sex. Nothing compares to sharing intimacy with one individual only and knowing that both people in the relationship are benefitting from it. Men think about sex nonstop, but women let it happen. He has never been able to understand the date-night concept. He thinks every night is a date night and that sex is a special gift.

This is a poem Bill wrote to his wife:

      L is for the LIGHT of my life

      O is for the ONCE is a lifetime

      V is for the VOW I will keep

      E is for the EVERY day I will love you

Bill's parents divorced when he was very young. At age fifteen, he and his sister moved out and he started his own business. This forced him to learn about finances at an early age. He is perplexed by the fact that certain cultures handle subjects of money, sex, and life's wisdom so differently. He didn't learn what an IRA or 401K was until he was older. Certain topics like money, sex, and faith weren't talked about in the open. When Bill had his own children, he created a "business contract" with them regarding how they would handle sex, drugs, drinking, and so on. After all had signed the contract, he posted it on the fridge. Then he told his children he would be there if anything ever happened to them. He asked his girls to remember that not only would they be hurting themselves but they would be hurting him as well if they broke the contract..

This Mosaic Man has always been interested in science. In fact, his first vocational goal was to be a doctor, dentist, or surgeon. But his sense of wanting to help others led him in a different direction. Early on, when a friend asked Bill how important family was to him, Bill had answered, "Everything." "Then medicine is not for you," his friend had replied. Medicine and insurances were changing in the eighties, and parents who wanted time for their children and family should forget about medicine as a vocation. "Be a priest of faith, and love Christ," was the advice he received. Eventually, his character was tested and brought to a place to observe three bodies—two men and one woman. It was as a funeral home. That is where he realized he could handle blood and could give to the care of people. Bill studied one year of pre-med and then moved on to Mortuary Science at PACE University. Common sense or street smarts can serve a person better than just a formal education, he believes.

This Mosaic Man is not politically active. Yes, he votes, but according to individual issues, not by party.

LOVE IS everything!

Bill thinks it's important to listen to others and that in addition to using one's brain, heart, and inner voice, people should listen to their gut!

To the little boy within, Bill says, "It took you too long to listen to your gut!"

D R .   M

MD, Internal Medicine

TODAY'S GIFT

Dr. M definitely relates to the Kaleidoscope Woman. NOW, that is. In her youth, she didn't feel like she was good enough. Her father was a typical old Yugoslavian man, who was very machismo. He was not emotionally attached and demanded that Dr. M always "be better." She did not receive the love from him that she deserved. In school, she was voted the best athlete and most likely to reach goals, but her father only saw her worth when she received her report card.

Dr. M's family consists of her wonderful kids—a daughter and a son, ages fifteen and eighteen, respectively. Her daughter is quite beautiful and developed beyond her age. Her son is a clear thinker and practical. Her family now is exactly as it's supposed to be. Dr. M is interested in helping young people stay addiction-free.

In her youth, Dr. M was rigid, OCD, complaining, and judgmental. Today, she is floating, loves people, and has developed the ability to ask personal questions about lives, fears, joys, and intimate moments. Of course, it's the patient who opens the door, one patient at a time. It is important to live in the moment, finding peace and joy.

To the little girl in this Kaleidoscope Woman, she says, "You are more than good enough!" Women search for approval from their fathers, and she searched for approval from her husband of eighteen years, who, much like her father was very structured and controlling. Also as with her father, she was never good enough for her husband. Her kids were born in New York, and her former husband was never accountable. He was too busy to deal with every day issues. In 2004, she saw the red flags in her marriage and moved to Florida.

Enlightenment excites Dr. M. She likes the fact that she is able to be and create anything she wants to be. She doesn't have to be a strict mother and can talk to people in the office. She likes learning about them and their lives.

Faith inspires Dr. M. It holds her life together; it's the glue and the battery. It also recharges her. She is a Christian who was raised in an Orthodox church and baptized in a Christian church. Her mother was a very religious and Bible-toting Christian. Faith is not about the fear of God, she'd say. God is love, we are all sinners, and God is OK with that. He has saved Dr. M many times in her life from catastrophic moments.

At age five, she recalls her parents fighting, and at some point she developed a dislike for men. Dr. M chose men in lesser positions than her and never questioned their insecurities.

This Kaleidoscope Woman doesn't let many people close to her. Perhaps four or five people are in her inner circle in addition to her four sisters. One sister is very dominating and another is free-spirited. Her young family environment in Arizona was toxic; it included addiction and bad marriages. In the last six years of her marriage, her husband lost his job and didn't feel the need to work because Dr. M was earning $350k, even though he had always been a hard worker. Today, she doesn't care what her father or ex-husband think.

Dr. M is now starting to take care of her health. She is diet-conscious, though she was formerly addicted to sleeping pills and diet pills and dependent on pills such as Ritalin. During those years, her husband bought her clothing and was very possessive of her. In her youth, she was a tomboy and considered not very feminine. Today, she wears heels every chance she gets, even while seeing patients.

This Kaleidoscope Woman does not have her finances together. She gives too much to others, but when she shops, she visits TJ Max and Marshalls rather than the malls. She loves giving to her kids. When she was married, she took over the finances. She took over the supposed man's role, which her ex-husband agreed to at the time. However, being Latin, he couldn't handle the role reversal.

Today, Dr. M is very sexual. It wasn't always that way. She took one year off from having sex after the divorce. Drinking and pills did not make her happy. She was devastated and torn apart. She was also angry. Toward the end of her marriage, she wound up having an affair with a man who did pay attention to her, but she paid the price by having her ex-husband say very cruel and demeaning things about her. In 2013, she hit rock bottom—no job, no kids, no self-respect. She felt lost! Then her spirituality shifted!

Dr. M's education took place in the Dominican Republic. It was a humbling experience. Some surgeries there were performed with no anesthesia. Sometimes patients had no money. And the hospital she volunteered in paid her with a meal. Dr. M thinks that children in the United States, especially millennials, need a slap to wake them up! Be humble in your learning, she counsels. If Dr. M had not become a doctor, she probably would have become a photographer. In her youth, she was very good at portrait and nature photography and even made money doing it. But, again, she was not good enough. Her experience in Santo Domingo was interesting because she didn't realize that a very tall blonde woman in the middle of primarily short black people would definitely stand out.

This Kaleidoscope Woman has never voted. She doesn't like Trump and doesn't like the liberal side of politics. She believes we are so tribal-like and divided by color, race, and gender, but she herself feels neutral. When she turns on CNN and hears all the bickering, she believes there are more fish to fry. Nobody talks about the death toll in the United States. That is something to talk about, she thinks.

Medicine in this country needs to change. Insurance companies are greedy, and pharmaceuticals are drug cartels. If she can give a pill to help a patient or take away one pill, she believes she's done a good job. Dr. M is moving more into alternative medicine—more into preventive medicine with focus on diet, exercise, and stress management.

She identifies with Blue. Every time she got in trouble as a child, she would go lie under a weeping willow and stare at the blue sky through the branches.

When Dr. M was eighteen years old, she placed second in the Miss Serbia contest. She couldn't say this then, but now she can say, "I feel I am the winner today in more ways than one!"

LOVE IS everywhere with God in your life. We Live, but it is not everything. The soul is what matters. Keep spirituality the drive of your life, and toss Ego away!"

To the little girl within herself, Dr. M says, "Thank you for never leaving me … and now we will really have fun!"

F O R T

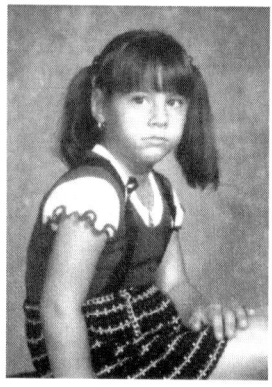

Mortgage Loan Officer

NEVER TOO LATE

Fort definitely identifies with the Kaleidoscope Woman, although she has changed so much over the years. She gives all of herself to whatever or whomever she is involved with. Especially to people she loves. This woman usually gives more than she receives. She feels she must learn to be a little more selfish. Perhaps it is being a firstborn child that makes her want to care for everyone. Her mom is her first priority and has a strong relationship with her. She also had a good relationship with her father, and in general, her relationships with her siblings are good. Fort is the person in the family who generally sacrifices and compromises more than the others, because she does not have children. As she gets older, she realizes that she continues to want to give more.

People inspire and move this woman, especially those who've had to overcome struggles on their way to achievements. Her mother and father are prime examples.

Green is this Kaleidoscope Woman's favorite color, but white is the aura that she identifies with and loves. Though green represents money, she has never been driven by money. She loves the purity and innocence of children and loves that they don't know about good and evil. They speak with no filter . . . so purely. White is innocence.

Fort will let people into her life who allow her to be who she is—people who accept her for the good, the bad, the ugly and the sensitive. She now loves who she is; it has only taken her forty-six years to get to this point.

As is true for many women, her number one priority is family. Perhaps it's because they are more important to her than she is to them. Again, she has no children, and family has become her world. Her mom still is her number one priority.

"You can count your true friends with one hand," her father had told Fort when she was young, and that is true for her now; she doesn't have many close friends—just a handful. Some time may pass when she doesn't see her friends often, but then when she does run into them, she feels like she's just talked to them yesterday. She used to think that friends could disappoint her, but she has learned to keep quality in her friendships. Some of her friends she adores and would do anything for.

Not very religious but very spiritual is how this woman relates to her faith. She believes that "something" brings us to the people in our life. Something out there knows everyone serves a purpose. An example in her life is the fact that her first and second husbands had the combined middle names of her present soulmate. Crazy! She married her first husband for freedom and the second husband hoping she would find tranquility, but it took finding her soulmate to find true love.

"No surgery or Botox on this face!" Fort believes in doing what makes her feel comfortable and keeps her looking good, but she will not go under the knife on her face. She has always taken care of herself, but at this time she is following more of a vegetarian food plan, and it's helping her body feel great! She used to exercise excessively but not anymore, although she still remains active. This woman will spend on creams and lotions but not surgery!

"Sex is great!" for this Kaleidoscope Woman. She has always been a sexual being who shares and enjoys exercises and fun. She has been open to experimenting with only a few men. Her soulmate is one of them. She is so comfortable with everything about him that she can be on a different level than ever before.

In previous relationships, Fort had to work very hard to take care of the household. She always felt she had to work because if she didn't, things would not be taken care of. This is the first time in her life that it's truly a financial partnership. EVERYTHING with him is a partnership . . . financially, sexually, and emotionally. Her partner handles the money because he is the CPA of the family, but she's the one who makes certain the bills are paid. At first, this arrangement felt foreign to her because she wasn't responsible for everything, but now she enjoys the partnership of her mate.

It's important to this Kaleidoscope Woman to have an academic as well as a street education. She knows many people without a college degree who are very smart. Her mom is a perfect example. It takes a balance of different types of education to succeed in life.

"OH . . . politics turns me off!" Fort does not find politics interesting. While she knows what's going on in the world, she finds it damages relationships. Opinions are OK, but nowadays she feels people get obsessive about politics, and it's not healthy. She prefers not to talk about it.

Through a friend of her father, Fort became involved in the mortgage business. Over twenty-five years of working as a mortgage loan officer has brought her some happy times and some not so happy. Her ultimate goal is to continue working in mortgages for a few more years and then go into the CPA practice with her soulmate. He needs good staff, and she would love to work with her partner.

If she could do something differently, she would live alone for a while. She didn't get a chance to travel because she never lived alone . . . wait, perhaps she could count the two months before meeting her soulmate. She recommends living alone and finding yourself because we have a tendency to conform to other people's wishes for our lives before our own.

To the little girl within, Fort says, "Love you first. You can't be with someone without loving yourself. Never settle!"

B O B B Y

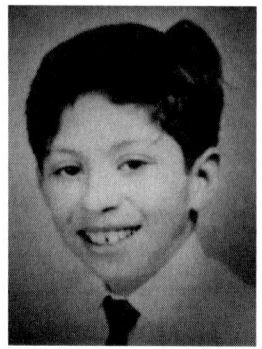

CEO/President

Florida Renaissance Festival

Actor

A FESTIVAL FOR ALL TIMES

LOVE IS the most important thing in our lives.

"Extremely important" is how this Mosaic Man describes family. He came from a broken home and a divorced family, and at that time—when he was five years old—divorce was not condoned. In fact, people looked down upon it. He had to lie a lot. When he was in eighth grade, a Christian Brother who was not compassionate told Bobby, "You will get married once and stay married."

Bobby was born and raised a Catholic. He remained Catholic until about 1977 when he was thirty years old and couldn't find a church that moved him. He is no longer a Christian nor connected to any particular church or congregation (he prefers no labels) but considers himself very spiritual. Bobby believes in the Apostles' Creed: "I believe in one God, the Father Almighty, Creator of heaven and earth and of all things visible and invisible." As the creed says, he believes in One God . . . whether that God is called Mother Nature, Buddha, or Allah. He also prays and believes that the power of prayer is in us all.

Yes, Bobby is healthy and active. He was always athletic, and played tennis and racquetball. Growing up, chronic asthma limited him, but he didn't pay attention to the doctors and pushed the envelope.

Sex is an important component in Bobby's life. In this country, sex carries a stigma, however. In Europe, you see topless beaches and perhaps Hollywood has a part to play with portraying women as too sexy or glamorous in the states.

Though this Mosaic Man grew up in the ghettos of New York, he was never out of work. At about twenty-one years of age, when Bobby moved to Los Angeles, he really didn't know the value or concept of making money work for a person. Instead, he lived from gig to gig. Now that he is successful financially, he has people who help him with his finances.

Bobby has always been a loner. He has taken the road less traveled. He's fifty-five and not married, but he's never uncomfortable going to dinner or the theater alone. He's also never hung out with the boys but is blessed with a handful of good friends. Of course, like many people, Bobby has been hurt by people he thought were friends but who were nowhere to be found in his time of need.

Both the street and formal college have educated Bobby. He wouldn't want his children to go through what he has seen or been through on the streets, however. His father and brother were street guys too. His dad had only a second-grade education, and his brother never finished high school. They had emphasized to Bobby, who was the baby of the family, the importance of finishing high school and college, which Bobby did. He then got a great job as a computer specialist in Los Angeles and lived an adventurous life at a singles' complex with tennis courts, restaurants, Movie Theater, library, basketball courts, and Jacuzzi. But he eventually left this wonderful life for the world of music.

Music has always been a part of Bobby's life, partly because his mom constantly listened to music in the house. There was a record store across the street, and he started a collection of forty-five records, developing an eclectic taste in music. He used to buy everything from country music to classical, and when he got his first record player, he listened to pop music as well. One day when he was nine years old and walking to school, he passed a furniture store with a bin of record albums for sale for mere pennies, and he added those albums to his collection.

Bobby sang in a church choir from the age of about eight. He sang for many years. Even today, he loves hearing many voices singing in the choir.

When this Mosaic Man was about thirteen years old, the flu kept him sick at home. Looking for something to do, he taught himself guitar. Later, at age sixteen, he started his first band. At eighteen, he began playing in night clubs, which helped put him through college.

Before becoming the CEO and President of the Florida Renaissance festival, Bobby started by producing music festivals—the Hollywood jazz festival and the first Hispanic festival in Broward County. He began to develop a great reputation and was part of an organization that asked him to develop a special annual event—his idea of a medieval festival. Three months before the event, however, the financers pulled the plug. He was devastated because he was penniless. Two years later, he did it on his own, and, as they say, the rest is history.

Being an actor, Bobby loves all kinds of movies, from *E. T.* to *Star Wars* to *Schindler's List.* He loves animation and dramas.

If Bobby were to do anything over again, he would learn to address his attention deficit disorder. His inability to read was very frustrating to him, but he wishes he had learned the importance of reading; he learned the importance of music in his life but only read for business. He thinks that held him back.

To the little boy within, Bobby says, "You've done the best you can with what you had!"

C L A U D I A

Artistic Theater Director

THE THINGS WE LEARN

Claudia believes we are magnets who draw in energies that other people possess. She is likable and caring, and when she was very young, a teacher called her effervescent. The teacher was stern-looking but had great depth of character. This Kaleidoscope Woman is strong, positive, and striving to be more humble, because she feels she has been blessed with so many talents and understanding that she would not want to be perceived as lacking humility. She truly admires Mother Teresa, who had patience and great humility.

Purple is probably the color of choice for this woman because it is one of the cozy colors and also elevates the spirit. In addition, Claudia identifies white light as a spiritual aura.

Knowledge and wisdom are what inspire Claudia. When she was a little girl, she was interested in everything and wanted to learn everything. She believes that knowledge brings wisdom, and was inspired by what she has achieved during her life and that makes her feel good. We are all put here to do something special, and it is up to us to find out what that is. Be the best of whatever you are, she advises. In order to make a difference in life, you have to do something that is outstanding in some field.

This Kaleidoscope Woman lets people who she can learn from into her life. The qualities of life are counted in the people we know. Learn those qualities.

LOVE IS a gift from God.

Claudia has known most of her friends for many years. She recently lost a roommate from college after a friendship of over sixty years. She has another friendship of fifty years and counts about five or six other friends to be very close. She stayed in touch with a gentleman who she studied voice with and got him a job on a cruise ship, but he has since passed away.

"Go for it!" were the words of Claudia's family. Her parents were wonderful and wanted Claudia and her older brother and sister to excel at what they wanted to be. "You can be anything you want, and if you have the passion for something, throw yourself into it!" they said. Her parents arranged classical piano lessons for her brother, who could, in one minute, turn around from playing Rachmaninoff to playing the boogey bogey. Her brother, Eddie, was the popular one, and little Claudia, who was ten years younger, wanted to be just like Eddie. He would play notes on the piano and ask Claudia, then four years old, to repeat them vocally; she replied with perfect pitch. Eddie was the one who told her parents to be sure Claudia studied with a good voice teacher, and they did. At dinner, Claudia's dad was always pushing to hear her sing.

Faith is number one in this Kaleidoscope Woman's life. The other day she passed the marquee of a church, which read, "In the beginning God." It brought Claudia to tears. Growing up, she would never dream of doing anything that would shame her family. She was strong and wouldn't do anything reprehensible or be less than her parents thought she was. In high school, kids road around in cars, drank beer, and smoked cigarettes, but Claudia always thought it was silly to burn a paper; she would rather have the money. Claudia believes in guardian angels; she believes they are on your shoulder, and, in addition to Heavenly bodies, she believes angels exist right here on earth to give us more strength.

Claudia believes that "Our sickness gives us more strength. You have to have strength to get through life and illness." There is definitely a reason Claudia survived three cancers, a kidney removed, and congestive heart failure. She would never have known about her heart issues if she hadn't been exercising and bending over to touch her toes; It was then that she realized her ankles and calves were huge. On August 15 (she remembers the date), she went to the clinic because she was worried about her physical condition. She registered with the receptionist and waited one hour. She now knows she was having a heart attack, was going to faint, and no one cared. She finally drove herself to the Northwest Medical Center and collapsed. They removed two gallons of fluid from her body. There are many ways to good health, Claudia believes; doctors and surgery are not the only methods for this woman. "It's a way of living!"

"The more you know, the better you will be," Claudia says. Learning was always easy for this Kaleidoscope Woman. She learned much in life and class and didn't have to study and didn't have to unlearn poor language skills. Her mom was an avid reader, and her father was very bright. Claudia received excellent grades in school and was a member of the National Honor Society. In high school, she mentored younger students. Both formal and common sense knowledge is important, she says. Common sense comes from living life and is also inherited.

At this time is her life, this Kaleidoscope Woman in not interested in sex. She was married twice, one of those times to a compulsive alcoholic and abusive man. He is the father to her children, and she used to think he could change. The second time, she married an unbalanced womanizer.

Claudia always knew she wanted to be an opera singer. So for fifteen years, she studied and learned. Her mom was a self-taught pianist who never felt she was good enough. Claudia wanted to be different. She had a wonderful career with five years in a professional opera company. She is happy with her professional life and believes there have been many fortunate accidents.

To Fellow Kaleidoscope Women, Claudia says, "Learn from experiences OR have self-pity and wallow in it!"

Claudia has been around the world five times and loves bringing happiness to other people's lives. For her, that is "The Music of Life!"

To the little girl within, Claudia says, "Don't be afraid to reach out and learn everything that interests you. Be kind, understanding of other people's problems. Give good educated advice. Achieve things that interest you, and then share with others. Have a strong faith in God, and love your country. Keep your faith, and your faith will keep you!"

CHAPTER TWELVE

VERONICA

Quality Assurance Manager

BEHIND THE SCENES

Yes, Veronica identifies with being a Kaleidoscope woman. She is genuine, crazy, loveable, a musician, a mother, and very creative.

This woman is inspired and moved by her children and love. Only genuine people and people who want to be loved hold a pace in Veronica's life.

Veronica has fears, but she faces and tackles them! Gold is the essence and aura of this Kaleidoscope Woman, because it is bright and beaming.

Veronica's immediate family comes first in her life. If you want to be loved, she is here for you. If you don't want to be loved, she's emotional and true enough to respect that. Veronica will always make time for friends if they want to be loved.

Faith is the foundation of this woman's life. She is a Christian and a true believer.

Veronica is beginning to focus on her health again. True, she goes up and down with her eating habits and has fallen off the wagon a few times, but she is ready to face what she has to do.

Love is the essence of sex for this Kaleidoscope Woman; three times a week is a nice schedule for her.

Financially, Veronica is self-taught and is learning to be more responsible with money. While she believes financial roles change in relationships, at this time she and her husband share the responsibilities 50/50.

"Very, very, very important!" is how this woman describes education, although she has struggled with finishing her own formal education; she has stopped and started before completing her degree.

Veronica thinks law and politics are touchy subjects, so she will reserve her opinions on those topics.

Returning to the medical field is not something she has to think about, because the work comes easy to her. Other fields she has spent time in include international business, education, travel, and entertainment.

LOVE IS taking a chance.

To the little girl within, Veronica says, "Don't stop trying . . . You can do it! Love you first!"

M I K E   L

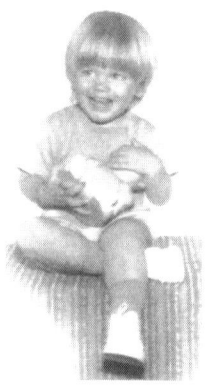

Broker Associate
Managing Director
Author

WALKING HAPPY

Mike is definitely a type A personality—competitive and sports-oriented. He believes in a team-comradery philosophy. He is patient with his children but finds it difficult to deal with adults who show excessive stupidity.

NO phobias for this Mosaic Man. Although, he is concerned about whether he will be able to always provide for his family at their current lifestyle. Oh, and he's maybe not too comfortable in the dark woods without a way out.

Money motivates Mike. He is inspired by trying to do what makes him and his family happy and by surrounding himself with happy people. He believes it's important to have friends who are loyal, because their loyalty will be returned. It's also good to have friends with common interests as well as people you can trust. At one point in Mike's life, he had many friends, but as he gets older, he finds his circle of friends getting smaller. Mike has about four men who fall into his circle, with whom he is very close. So close that he would put his life in their hands. Mike's philosophy on friendship is that close friends try not to let anything get in between them. Of course we are all human and sometimes it's better to meet up once in a while. We all make mistakes, but to Mike, a good friend is someone who you can discuss a problem with and then work it out, fix it.

This sports fanatic loves golf, baseball, football, and hockey. As a young man, Mike played hockey for seventeen years in Michigan for a city league. His dad was a little league coach and got Mike, at age seven, into baseball, hockey, and golf. Mike began playing recreational ball and then competitive ball.

LOVE IS "my children." You need patience to fully love someone.

To this Mosaic man, family is number one. He has good relationships with everyone in his family—Mom, Dad, sister, and brother. They all live in Michigan, but he speaks with his mom on a daily basis.

Faith has been instilled in the family. In one week, Mike's eight-year-old daughter will be celebrating her first holy communion, and the entire family will be there to celebrate.

Growing up middle class, this Mosaic man didn't want for much. Mike's dad left high school in the ninth grade, and worked for thirty-five years to support his family of five children. At a very young age, Mike had a concept of money, but, because his parents gave him everything he needed, he didn't learn about really dealing with finances until his first job. Today, Mike handles the grocery shopping, cooking, and ninety percent of the finances in the household. He wants to continue to provide for his family.

Health is also important to Mike. He exercises and goes to the gym but fluctuates now and then with junk food.

"Sex is an important part of any relationship," he says, but as some married people know, the longer you are together, the less sex there is. Today, Mike has two girls.

Mike believes that a formal education will definitely help a person attain success in life, but street smarts and working hard will also further your education and road to success. Although neither his dad nor his mom had a college education, they definitely provided a good life for their family. Learning a trade can also be important. Both forms of education are important. Today, Mike notes, children are being taught where to search for the answers instead of memorizing and knowing the answers.

Mike is not politically active, but he does vote in every election. His decisions boil down to how policies will affect him and his family. He thinks that people who don't vote shouldn't try to put their two cents into how the country is run. He is a registered Republican while his entire family are Democrats.

Three of Mike's top movies are *Saving Private Ryan, The Avenger Marvel Comic Series,* and *Old School.*

Business management and communications were Mike's majors in school. He thought about going into the insurance business, but while he was still in Michigan, he formed a landscaping company with a partner. In 1993 he moved to Florida and worked part-time jobs to make ends meet. Intrigued by the idea of becoming a commodities broker, he took and passed his series three license test. For almost seven years, he worked with stocks as a commodities broker until he burned out. Yet, he knew he was strong at sales. Eventually a real estate office in Del Ray recruited him, and, as they say, the rest is history. This Mosaic Man now deals in millions of dollars' worth of real estate monthly.

To the little boy within, Mike says, "Follow your dreams, and don't take 'No, You Can't Do That' for an answer!"

CHAPTER FOURTEEN

JEWELL C.

Property Manager

OVERLOAD

Jewell identifies with being a Kaleidoscope Woman because she is on "Overload!" She is honest and has a great sense of humor and a very giving heart. She is always taking care of everyone else before herself and attributes that to being very motherly with everyone. This has not changed over time. And, oh yes, Cheetos cheese puffs are her thing!

Soft, mellow, bold, and passionate may appear to be opposites, but they represent the pink and red colors that Jewell identifies with. She is definitely a wild child!

Family is the number one priority in this woman's life. This woman is moved and inspired by her family and kids; they are the energy that keeps her moving forward. She has good relationships with them and feels she gets along with everyone, including some she shouldn't (smile). Yes, as a mother, she is a good listener and believes that you must let your children make mistakes but be there to catch them if they fall. She is always there for any issues the family wants to discuss.

She was raised in a rough environment; her mother married and divorced five times, and Jewell vowed that she would fight hard to not be like her mother. There were times when her family had no food, no power, and no bed, but they made it out ok. Jewell wonders if things might have turned out differently had her parents been strict with her.

Sometimes, Jewell is too trusting and lets too many people into her circle. But that is because she feels God gives her a purpose.

Jewell chooses not to have many friends in her life. She knows a lot of people but not as best of friends, because she's been hurt so many times and that has broken her trust. After leaving Florida twenty years ago, she continues to communicate with a very dear friend through Polo.

LOVE IS patient.

This Kaleidoscope Woman says "Big time" to the question of whether faith plays an important role in her life. She wouldn't be where she is today were it not for her faith. Jewell remembers seeking God at nine or ten years old. She would walk by herself to church every week—first a Baptist church and then a Catholic church. A little bit of this and that until now, where she is a Christian. She has learned that you don't have to go to church to believe in God.

For her age, Jewell is relatively healthy, though she does take medication for high blood pressure, and a growing health issue for her is severe allergies. In her twenties, Jewell had a hysterectomy but has been fine ever since. She gets a mammogram annually but has passed on the pap smear for the past twenty-five years.

Not until her late forties did this woman learn about finances. During her marriage of twenty-three years, her husband took care of the money. After their divorce, Jewell didn't know how to write a check. So she learned on her own. Today, with her present husband, who she adores, they handle the finances fifty-fifty.

"Ha Ha!! What about sex?" this Kaleidoscope Woman replies. When she was younger, she was not into sex because her first husband was sexually abusive. She experienced orgasm only after her divorce. "Nope!" no sex in thirteen years, she says. She doesn't miss sex as much as the cuddling and smooching part of being close to someone. She and her present husband sleep in separate beds because their bodies generate so much heat that they perspire.

Unfortunately, education was not a big thing for this Kaleidoscope Woman in her growing up years. She didn't graduate, because she was married and pregnant, plus she really didn't enjoy school subjects; they didn't excite or motivate her. In addition, she was made fun of in school. Classmates teased her because of her thin legs, large breasts, and Mickey Mouse ears. Some called her "Grand Tetons." Jewell believes there is a difference between notebook smarts and street smarts. Because the world can be so cruel, she thinks you wouldn't get very far without street smarts, which is how she was raised.

Jewell thinks most politicians are phony liars. For that reason, she follows politics but does not get involved in it; she doesn't want to associate with that. In her life, Jewell has gotten one ticket for speeding.

Oh my gosh, don't let this woman see a mouse or rat! She is also claustrophobic; no elevators or closed doors, please!

This Kaleidoscope Woman has worked at many jobs during her life, including a shoe repair shop, cleaning company, car dealership auction, and specialty printing. Now, as a property manager, she is mother to all the residents and builds relationships with all of them.

To the little girl within, Jewell says, "Be who you are, and be yourself. You are strong, and there isn't anything you can't do without patience and love!"

L I N D A

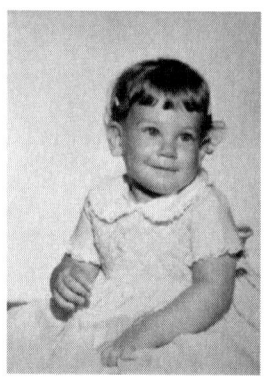

Reiki Master

A HIGHER VIBRATION

Linda is a Kaleidoscope Woman who is constantly morphing. She is a woman of many depths, flavors, colors, and layers who believes nothing is black and white. She is morphing like a butterfly, and the older she gets, the better her life is. She uses her senses and looks to move with confidence through life experiences. Through her energy field is her spiritual growth.

Love inspires this woman and is the driving force in her life. She is mother to all— nurturing to people and animals and providing loving support to everyone.

LOVE IS all encompassing. It is life's highest vibration in the universe.

Not being understood is a concern for Linda, as well as not meeting expectations of others. Public speaking also challenges this woman, but she moves with the flow through such uncomfortable situations. She's OK with tight spots but is not a fan of dark places. She has a phobia of heights if she not in a container, like a plane, for instance. But she reminds herself she has everything inside herself that she needs to conquer her fears.

This Kaleidoscope Woman lets very few people into her life. She has always been a woman of quality rather than quantity and values deep hearts and a true self. No BS version of friendship for her. She does not feel the need to compete and will let in those with no big egos and who are not guarded - people who will be friends forever. Linda appreciates people who are honest and will tell you if you're behaving like a jerk. Friends are people you can select and are very important.

Family is the core, or base, of life. They don't have to be biological. They are a vessel to learn from on this earth, and, together with friends, they create a family.

Linda was raised a Catholic but didn't rush into organized church because she didn't connect with it. Instead, she went in and out of churches until she found her spiritual path. "There is no man in the cloud that punishes," she says. She believes in the higher power that created this universe and has seen miracles based on positive thoughts. It all boils down to frequency. Your being will attract what you get. Vibrate in love, and faith will always follow.

This woman knows that the body is the house of the soul. It's important to take care of it. It's amazing how the body is a miraculous vessel and should be taken care of; drinking good water, fruits, veggies. Of course, Linda cheats once in a while, but life is a balance and pizza is okay in moderation if it makes you happy (smile).

Finances are something Linda wishes she had learned more about at an early age. Her mom definitely taught her to save, save, save and be frugal as she grew up. Concern about not having enough money led Linda to pursue a nine-to-five job in order to earn enough money to pay her bills and gain benefits, including insurance. Now she follows her soul's purpose as a Reiki Master. She loves what she's doing, but bank accounts are still crazy.

This Kaleidoscope Woman believes there is a gigantic difference between book smarts and formal education. She has earned her bachelor's degree in business and psychology, but it was more like a hobby for her. She believes that traditional schools are biased and teach what they want. Linda loves to learn and is like a sponge when it comes to knowledge. She is an avid reader and believes that students should be taught at an early age the skills to learn about nutrition, love, and spiritual skills. The best education is to backpack around the world, but street smarts carried her through life.

"Let it flow!" when it comes to sex for this woman. We are sexual beings, she says. For Linda, no color or gender has been a factor in her sexuality. She does feel there is a stigma about nudity in the United States, where it's a no-no. For Linda, fluid is the way to go.

Linda has zero interest in politics because the political world does not tap into love and politicians are not honest. If she were to get involved in politics, it would be for human and animal rights, including the rights of children and the elderly.

At this time in her life, Linda is morphing all over the place. She loves what she does, and even if it's one person at a time, she is happy giving people a loving, compassionate, and safe place following the soul's purpose. When she was younger, she fell into believing work, schoolwork, babies, and a corporate job was the path to take. When she hit thirty, with no children and divorced, she decided to spread her wings. She was miserable in the corporate world and knew there was more to life than that. She is developing personally every day.

During her off time, Linda does research for her clients and for herself to continue to learn and grow. Many of her books are self-help. Being a Taurus, she enjoys good meals, dining out, anything ocean-related, travel, and seeing new things. She absolutely loves to travel. She also enjoys sporting events, concerts, classical music, and anything pertaining to the arts, including feel-good movies like *The Notebook* and *Under the Tuscan Sun.*

To the little girl within, Linda says, "Believe in yourself to know that you are stronger than you could ever imagine. Embrace the divine inner soul that is the power behind your being."

L U I S A

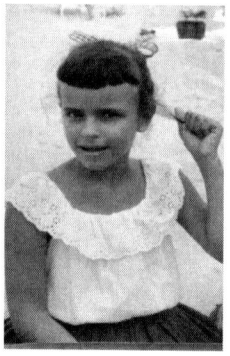

Visual Artist

STAYING IN THE PRESENT

Luisa absolutely identifies with the Kaleidoscope Woman. In reality, she believes, most females are multi-dimensional but are not aware of it because they only focus on the outward physical reality instead of the inside reality.

"Very emotional" is how Luisa describes part of her being. She likes to think of herself as someone with depth and she doesn't like the philosophy of "what you see is what you get!" She sees the meaning in things and likes to figure out what makes everyone an individual. Perhaps this has to do with her creative nature and the part of the brain that is more developed, as well as other factors. Luisa believes creative people are freer because they are not functioning within a box.

This Kaleidoscope Woman is more moved and inspired by what we don't see in this physical world than what we see. She's excited by the spiritual energy that makes things happen in the physical realm. She is stirred by the quantum world where all possibilities exist.

DO NOT put this woman in a room full of cockroaches or sharks; she loves to swim in the ocean but is constantly looking down to see if there are any sharks around.

Luisa will let people into her life that have "good energy." She must be comfortable being herself because she can't conform to others. Her friends are accepting, open-minded, and sensitive to more than what we can see. "It's all about those with good energy; they're cool and can chill!"

The blue throat chakra, which is responsible for our communication, is the color of choice for this Kaleidoscope Woman. The sky is also blue, and Luisa is inspired by all gametes of blue tones. Ironically and esthetically, there is not much blue in her house. In her home, she tends to be contemporary and has learned through her culture that blue resonates with her.

Being proud of a good education, Luisa returned to school in her forties and graduated with honors. She is proud that she walked away from the lucrative mortgage industry to pursue her career in the arts. She did it because it was important for her personal growth and not just about the money. "You can't take money with you! You really don't!" she emphasizes. Luisa is proud that she has invested in herself and her time rather than just material things. Being overworked and making money only means a person spends more, and that cycle is not easy to break.

Of course, family is very important to this Kaleidoscope Woman. "My families are the people who choose to hang out with me. My soul chooses the people I hang out with in this lifetime."

Luisa believes friends did not choose you as a soul before you incarnated. Rather, you consciously chose them. She has some friends who are not blood, but a few have been around forever. While she considers some people to be good friends, she is not a groupie. Her philosophy is have few friends but good ones.

LOVE IS the absence of fear.

This Kaleidoscope Woman is not involved with organized religion. Having an intermediary does not make sense to her. Luisa believes that God, and what people believe in, is energy. It is a form of creative energy that all people have the ability to get in touch with on their own. "Be intuitive on your own," she advises. She thinks some people need organized religion. "If it works for them, fine, but it doesn't work for me" (chuckle). . . . "Too constraining!"

Managing finances was not something Luisa was taught. Her father was a bohemian and didn't teach his children about handling money. Throughout her life, finances have been challenging for her. It's curious that this Kaleidoscope Woman has never been that interested in or obsessed about money, because she felt she never lacked anything. Her family wasn't rich, but neither were they poor. Her dad was carefree and a nut: "A great nut!"

Luisa thinks formal education is a really good base to have because it's important to train the brain to think in different ways. Formal education develops your writing and reading skills, she believes. You must also research on your own or you will be limited. Some people have done a great job at self-education. Academia gives you certain structures and parameters. It forces you to ask, can I do this? A good education helped her gauge who she was intellectually. Luisa thinks it's funny that in school she was all over the place with her interests and didn't care; but she wondered why she had certain skills. Other things interested her at that time.

Important, but not the main thing in life, is this Kaleidoscope Woman's feelings about sex. Sexually, Luisa is extraverted, but it's not the focal point in her life. She enjoys a sexual relationship with the right person but has never been driven by it. If she likes someone enough, she will have sex with them; he has to care. Having sex has nothing to do with morality for her; she really has to care about the guy. She doesn't judge others who don't approach sex like this, but she must have an emotional attachment to engage sexually.

Luisa knows that politics affects lives; she is aware of events around her but does not campaign for anyone. She is very disappointed in politics because it is not currently producing politicians at a level of consciousness that she would like to see. When our society is better, our politics will be better too, she says. As a society, we need reflection. Companies donate so much money to campaigns, and we must find a way to stop big money from running politics. Luisa is very frustrated with politics. She feels there is no true empathy for people in the political world; it's all about the ego—the politician and power. "It's very sad!"

Being a visual artist, this Kaleidoscope Woman was not happy in the business world. She now loves her life and enjoys immensely what she does as a professional artist. She feels balanced, and her energy has evened out. It's important for her to create, but the public relations aspect of the business is a pain. She uses social media to promote her work and has been invited to many prestigious shows. Luisa has decent collections and is proud to be a working artist. Her work can be seen in hotels, established galleries, and cruise ships. She has recently been invited to attend an art fair in Lebanon.

To the little girl within, Luisa says, "Be fearless and go get it! You can do it! There is nothing you can't do if you set out to accomplish it!

S T E P H E N

Composer/Poet/Artist

FROM ACROSS THE POND

Stephen is an intensely loyal man who is also perceptive and extremely creative. He is a curious individual who is detail-oriented and infinitely patient.

This Mosaic Man was born in Birmingham, England, and came from a family of six. Generally speaking, Stephen had an idyllic childhood. During his younger years, the family had a close nucleus. He remembers fondly as the oldest child how they use to go on walks together through the villages and country lanes.

Stephen's life changed when he was about eleven years old and heard his mother crying in the other room. He found out his father was having an affair with a neighbor. At about twelve years old, he followed his dad and confronted him, only to receive a beating from his father.

The incident turned out to be the scandal on the street, and eventually the family left the UK and immigrated to America. Today, Stephen is estranged from his family but wishes he had been more diplomatic after his mom's death.

At this time, Stephen has a clean bill of health, although he did have a bout with colon cancer and is in remission. He lost a great deal of weight due to the cancer and wishes he had more discipline to get back in shape. He's afraid he has let himself go.

This Mosaic Man has a tendency to not worry about money. As long as he has enough to take his girlfriend out for dinner, a show, or concert, he's okay. He's not a penny pincher and has never been a money person.

Artists, musicians, and poets are the people in Stephens's life—people who are friendly. Mundane people or zombies don't do it for this Mosaic Man.

Fear is not a part of the character of this man. He considers himself a survivor and will land on his feet. His mom used to tell him to always look like you know what you're doing, and no one will ever stop you.

Great works of art, music, writing, and painting are some of what inspires and moves Stephen. He can spend a full day just looking through catalogs, works of art, or music arrangements.

Stephen has studied at the Berkley School of Music, Broward Community College, and Atlantic Vocational School. He thinks there is a major difference between a formal education and street smarts. Street smarts will serve you better than a paper degree, he says, and a formal education can be limiting and overrated.

Sex plays a major role in Stephen's life. He is a sensuous person and uses touch and feel as methods of observation. "Sex is intuitive," says Stephen and likes to feel that he's met on equal terms by his partner.

This Mosaic Man has always been politically active. In fact, he considers himself an activist. He believes there should be full disclosure in politics and that the facts should be presented in such a way that we, the people, can assess the truth. Since the last election and for the past two years, Stephen feels like he has been in a bad dream. Everything that could go wrong politically is going wrong.

This Mosaic man has years of experience as a property manager of a country club, but he knows that this kind of work was counter to his grain. Music has always been his number one interest. As a child, Stephen's dad played harmonica, and when Stephen turned five, his dad taught him to play. He learned so quickly that everyone knew Stephen was a natural and had an ear for music.

Stephen's mom wanted him to be a violinist, but he was bullied in school about it. So he looked for a more "masculine" instrument and switched to trumpet. At eight and a half, Stephen was selected as best musician in the Brass Choral and moved into the County Orchestra in England. Eventually, he moved into the British Youth Orchestra. He left England at the height of Beatlemania. He could always relate to chorus, band, and art in high school in the United States. He got along well with his fellow students in his music class.

At Expo '67, Stephen represented the United States at the American Pavilion in Montreal; he was fifteen years old. By the time he was a teenager; he played drums in a band and did well. Eventually, he started playing in a rock and roll band, managed other bands, and recorded in a studio built in his garage. Then he earned a scholarship to

Berkley School of Music. At some point, he became bored and found himself drafted by the US Army. His music career came to a halt.

During basic training, Stephen developed double pneumonia, which, in hindsight, saved his life. While being hospitalized, he saw a poster about auditioning for the US Army Infantry Chorus; he auditioned and started performing at Fort Benning. During that time, he was asked to form a rock/jazz band called "Others First." This Mosaic Man left the army in 1973 for Los Angeles. He played many clubs and was compared to Cat Stevens. In 1975, he came to Fort Lauderdale and has played in bands and painted ever since. He knows how much work it takes to be in a band, but if a gig came his way, he would jump at it!

LOVE IS everything!

The hobbies of this Mosaic Man are aviation and aircraft model making.

Brazil (directed by Terry Gilliam), *After Midnight,* and *Vicky Christina Barcelona* (directed by Woody Allen) are some of Stephen's favorite movies.

A spiritual person is how Stephen describes himself. He is not into organized religion but considers himself a Christian who is still researching with the help of the writings of Ron Wyatt. He believes in reincarnation and feels he was a fighter pilot in a previous life.

To the little boy within, Stephen says, "Always do what you love, and it will never be work!"

J E W E L   R

Director of Operational Excellence

Certified Life Coach

Author

A JEWEL IN THE CROWN

Jewel is continually changing and evolving toward the woman she is purposed to be. Each situation, whether good or bad, propels her towards her destiny. She is strong, resilient, and steadfast in her ambitions. She has the unique ability to turn life challenges into learning experiences. She is virtuous and upright.

This woman is moved by God's unconditional love and kindness that is shown toward others. She is inspired by words of affirmation and selfless giving.

This Kaleidoscope woman has a fear of failure. As a result, she strives to face and overcome her fears so that it does not prevent her from living to her greatest potential.

Jewel is cautious about who she lets into her life. She is drawn to people who are positive and encouraging. She pulls away from people who are negative and draining.

Family is very important to this Kaleidoscope Woman. Family provides a framework of love and support, which mold and shape her character. Who she becomes in adulthood is a direct reflection of the family values instilled in childhood.

Friends play an essential role in the life of this Kaleidoscope Woman. They provide a feeling of connectedness and help the Kaleidoscope Woman successfully transition through the many seasons of life. True friendships are real and can sustain tough conversations. One of her favorite scriptures regarding friendship is Proverbs 27:6 (NIV): "Wounds from a friend can be trusted, but an enemy multiplies kisses."

Christian faith is the most important aspect of Jewel's life. It is the reason she exists, the center of her life. She realizes that God created her uniquely with gifts and talents to meet the needs of those in the world. She believes that only by seeking an intimate relationship with God can she successfully fulfill the calling that is on her life.

Health is a critical facet for this Kaleidoscope Woman. She understands that in order to be in good health, she must focus on physical, mental, and spiritual health. So she is intentional about maintaining wellness in each of these areas.

Sex plays a significant role in the life of this married Kaleidoscope Woman. She recognizes that sex is a gift from God for married heterosexual couples. She recognizes I Corinthians 7:3–5 (NIV): The husband should fulfill his marital duty to his wife, and likewise the wife to her husband. The wife does not have authority over her own body but yields it to her husband. In the same way, the husband does not have authority over his own body but yields it to his wife. Do not deprive each other except perhaps by mutual consent and for a time, so that you may devote yourselves to prayer. Then come together again so that Satan will not tempt you because of your lack of self-control."

This woman recognizes that being a good steward of her finances is a daily principle she must follow. She believes that all of her income comes from God. As a result, she cheerfully contributes a tenth of her income to her church. She strives to maintain minimum to zero debt. She pays her bills on time, and she has a short- and long-term financial investment plan.

Education breeds opportunity is what Jewel believes. Education equips her with knowledge and skills to change the world. She is deliberate in her pursuit of education. She excels through dedicated application of key learnings.

This Kaleidoscope Woman understands the value of politics and law but recognizes the flaws and unfairness that exist within this structure. Many times, she is heartbroken to see the disparity in treatment among different races and classes of people. She prays for political leaders who make decisions in the best interest of all people. She prays for laws and enforcement agencies that are fair and just to all people.

The Kaleidoscope Woman knows that she was created for a specific purpose. All that she does professionally is purposeful and done to glorify God. She uses her profession as a means to demonstrate the love of Christ in her treatment of others. She uses her profession to illustrate the excellence of Christ in the quality of her deliverables. She operates in the spirit of excellence. She remains humble throughout her professional career. She gives God all the glory and honor for her accomplishments and successes.

To the little girl within, Jewel says, "The thing you fear is often what you need to overcome to walk in purpose."

CHAPTER NINETEEN

GILDA

Lawyer

TO TELL THE TRUTH

Yes! Gilda identifies with the Kaleidoscope Woman. She is somebody who can relate to many people. She not only relates to different kinds of experiences that cross her life but she can take situations that present themselves to her and work with her strengths to overcome them or to help others overcome situations.

Yellow is the color that reflects this Kaleidoscope Woman's aura. It balances her surroundings and is able to relate to them.

Family, friends, and her work inspire Gilda. She has a desire to do well in this world and help others. This Kaleidoscope Woman only allows family and close friends into her life. Needless to say, family is her number one priority, with friends coming in second.

Gilda's philosophy of faith is not based on religion. Judaism does not govern her life regarding what to do or how to be. Faith is doing the best with what has been given to a person by God. We are born with characteristics and traits and must do the best with what we have been given. Faith plays an important third priority in her life.

This Kaleidoscope Woman tries to live a healthy life. Family and faith are important to good health, and together they play a big dynamic in life.

Ah sex . . . yes and no! Not in love with it right now. Sadly, at this time, sex is not at the forefront of Gilda's brain. It's an important component, however, of maintaining a healthy relationship with her significant other. It's a part of the circle of a relationship with him but not a priority for her right now.

Finances are important as a means to provide for the family. She believes that she works hard to give her kids what they deserve. However, she doesn't believe that finances are number one or two. Money is a means of providing, and she will not sacrifice the balance of making money with motherhood. She will try to give her children everything but will not miss out on anything while doing so.

Education is extremely important to this Kaleidoscope Woman. She was raised to be the best you can be in school. "To make something of yourself" resonated and stayed with her through life. Gilda believes education opens many doors and gives people knowledge they might otherwise not have gained. It gives a woman a sense of independence, she says. There is a difference between a formal education and a street education for Gilda. A street education is a powerful tool to have because it gives common sense that can't be learned in school. The best of both worlds is the perfect combination.

Gilda believes it is important to exercise the right to vote and to know what's going on around you. She believes it's good to have a general understanding of present-day politics. As long as she knows what's going on in general, she thinks that's sufficient.

This Kaleidoscope Woman is a lawyer. She represents different facets of hotels, hospitals, centers, and stores where injuries on the property take place. She handles lawsuits and/or trial litigation on behalf of these business entities involved in TORT-related lawsuits. She likes her work and enjoys finding the strengths in her cases and working the case up based on those strengths.

LOVE is universal.

To the little girl within, Gilda says, "Be the best you can be!"

CHAPTER TWENTY

RICHARD C

Actor

A GRATEFUL HEART

LOVE IS a many splendored thing!

Richard does not hesitate to take care of himself. After triple bypass surgery, he does not put off until tomorrow what he can do today! He believes one ounce of prevention is worth a pound of cure. He does watch his cholesterol, but he's fine and in tip-top shape today. His health is his number-one priority.

This Mosaic man is very close with most of his family and extended family. Unfortunately, he is estranged from his youngest brother. Richard thrives on his contact with all the family units. His father was an artist and his mother a nurse and performer. He was close with his dad, who passed away when Richard was in his thirties. At that time, Richard became even closer with his mom. The two of them moved down to Florida together over twenty-nine years ago and were inseparable. He doesn't like to lose touch with the family because they are his number two priority in life.

Faith play an important role is Richards's life. He tries to follow the traditions passed down to him, but he is not religious. He is a member of the synagogue in upstate New York and has arranged his burial rights in "boot hill." He even has his stone ready next to his mom and dad. He always wanted to write what he wants on his base, and he has done that.

Richard has not always handled finances well, but he is doing better at it now. Other than when his mom was alive, Richard has always handled the finances.

Friendships run very deep with Richard. He still has friends from elementary school and college, most of which have effervescent personalities. One of best friends is from first grade. Yes, Richard has an eclectic group of friends.

"Enjoy it while you can" is Richard's philosophy about sex. He has never had a committed partner but admires people who do.

This Mosaic Man does not belong to any political club, but as he gets older he is more distraught about the political scene. Things have to get better than they are now.

Richard's hobbies are genealogy, photography, and presidential trivia.

Water, whether it is the ocean or the pool, brings fear to this man.

Richard's all-time favorite film is *All about Eve*; *Moonstruck* and *Mildred Pierce* follow close behind.

This Mosaic Man has worked in banking and on Wall Street '81–'87. He was also a substitute teacher, a patient advocate, and a volunteer ambulance worker. In high school in the ninth grade, Richard got the acting bug. His first audition was to play the part of a man who spoke funny because he had a cold. As fate would have it, Richard was sick with a cold when he auditioned, and of course, he got the part. His biggest role in high school was Tevye in *Fiddler on the Roof.* He also created a talent show to raise funds to go on a trip to Washington, DC. His nickname was Barko Puchie. As part of Marquee Productions in Florida, he played the Rabbi in *Fiddler on the Roof,* which toured throughout Florida.

This Mosaic Man is grateful for where he is today and carries with him the following quote by Marcus Aurelius: "When you arise in the morning, think of what a precious privilege it is to be alive—to breathe, to think, to enjoy, to love."

To the little boy within, Richard says, "Don't be afraid to follow your heart. Enjoy life to the fullest, and don't worry what other people think of you. Be who you are!"

ALEXIS

Assistant to Artistic Theater Director

Entertainer

THIRD TIME IS THE CHARM

Alexis absolutely identifies with the Kaleidoscope Woman with all the facets to her life! And she now feels, at this stage of her life very surprised that she would use what she learned at eighteen years old. That makes you who you are today.

This Kaleidoscope Woman is friendly, outgoing, nurturing, warm, caring, and vibrant. Alexis is the unlimited cup, half-full kind of woman. "Life is too short to be negative!" she says.

Red is the color Alexis's aura because it is bold, exciting, vibrant, and passionate. It is a powerful and a feel-good color.

The only fear that Alexis faces is not being scripted. She has worked with scripts all her life and feels shaky when off script.

Her children and now her new grandson inspire and excite this woman. She's moved by the beautiful mountains of Colorado, corny love stories, hallmark movies, and seeing her daughter perform.

Alexis is very open to letting people into her life—sometimes too open. She accepts people unconditionally, and it doesn't faze her to let people into her heart. It's so special, she feels, to "let people in" that she feels she has known forever. It's nice when you see people only sporadically but it still feels like no time has passed since you've seen them.

Family is definitely the number-one priority to this woman. Alexis comes from an Italian family, where family has always come first, even in childhood. She has two sisters and one brother; Alexis is the baby.

Many friends are a part of Alexis's life. One of her friendships began when she was sixteen years old. Her friends are of different professions and ages.

Sex is different now after menopause, and it's not a priority for Alexis. Things like tenderness, hugging, cuddling, and kissing are more important than the act of sex.

Faith has always been a part of this woman's life. She was raised Catholic and attended Catholic elementary and high school. After finishing school, Alexis didn't attend church frequently. She is what you call a "C and E" Catholic, attending mass on Christmas and Easter. Six months ago, Alexis decided to marry her fiancé, Randy, and he wanted to get married in a church. Now they both attend St Stephen's church in Pompano Beach. They both love the pastor. He is down to earth and was married and divorced. Because of this, he puts the scripture into laymen's terms, making it useful for everyday life. The service is at 10:15 a.m. every Sunday. They will be holding a Unity Sand Ceremony on June 17. Randy has been married five times and Alexis 3. Alexis says, "This time we're gonna get it right!

All her life, Alexis has been on a yo-yo diet. She is Italian and loves to cook and eat. Weight Watchers is her go-to plan. At fifty-five, she is feeling better than ever. After years of gymnastics and martial arts, she realized that even with all the healthy habits, the strain from running, jumping, and heavy bags took a toll on her body. She looks back at photos when she was in her forties and thinks she looked like a skeleton and unhealthy. She is now "OK with feeling good and happy in her own skin!"

This Kaleidoscope Woman has a great relationship with finances. She learned to save when she worked at a bank at age eighteen. She had a bank book for every goal: vacation, Christmas, gifts, etcetera. She saved early in her life but regrets not putting anything into an IRA for the future. In her first marriage of fifteen years, her husband earned a great deal of money and she didn't have to worry about finances until he started overspending and they had to refinance their house. She should have paid closer attention because she doesn't budget well. In her new marriage, they will share a family account and have separate checking accounts.

Alexis's advice to her daughter was to go to college for a degree she could use later. So her daughter went out, followed in her mother's footsteps, and got her degree in Musical Theater. Alexis had to drop out of school after two years because she was having her children. She wanted to be a voice teacher, so she studied piano and voice.

Confrontation or arguments are not something Alexis will take part in. She is not active in politics and believes that "secret ballots" are secret for a reason. She doesn't want to explain.

This Kaleidoscope Woman started working as a bank teller, then became a supervisor and worked in banking for fifteen years. She has also worked as a massage therapist for eighteen years, an insurance broker, and—after graduating from broadcasting school—as a broadcaster on a local radio station.

Alexis has loved music and entertaining since she was six years old. She has been a professional vocalist, dancer, and actress for over thirty-five years. When the family moved to Florida from New York in 1970, there was nothing there—just open land. When the family would visit her father, her dad would have her sing for the family, along with his old 45 records. Her first microphone was her dad's plastic cigar holder, and at six years old she would sing, "I am woman, hear me roar!"

Fellow Kaleidoscope Women take note: Alexis would like to say, "Follow your dream!" Because she was afraid of not having money for her family, she never had the guts to do follow her own dream . . . so fuck it!

"I am happy to be a part of the Kaleidoscope Woman group," Alexis says. ". . . They are all Strong women!!"

To the little girl within, Alexis says, "Speak up and follow your dream! Don't be afraid to tell your feelings; hurt or whatever. People are not mind readers. They will keep doing it if you never tell them to stop."

CHAPTER TWENTY-TWO

MARIELLA

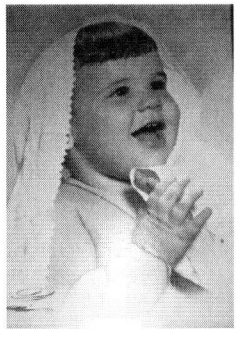

Fashion Designer

CELEBRATING MOMMY

This is Mariella describing herself; yes, Mariella is a Kaleidoscope Woman. Thanks to another Kaleidoscope Woman in my life—my mother—I luckily acquired her gifts of wisdom and the ability to influence and inspire others.

As a spiritual woman, a professional, a wife, a mother, a grandmother, and a mentor, I believe I have put myself and my life in complete balance, thus being able to achieve it all without forgetting the true meaning of this rainbow we call life.

My color representation is yellow and illuminates my thoughts daily. Believing in myself, my faith in the Almighty, the significance of our path, and the importance of caring and giving is what fulfills and motivates me every day; it allows my constant flow of inspiration.

I admire strong women, and my mother was my best teacher! She always taught me to ground myself and know that "no one is better than you, but you are not better than anyone." Those were her constant words, and they ring in my ears every day. This is what makes a woman see beyond her needs and care for the needs of others, but without ever taking away from herself.

I celebrate my mother . . . and all those women out there who have learned that life is a short jump that must be accomplished thoroughly and without fears!

Life is a kaleidoscope in itself. It's what moves us to accomplish the next; it is what teaches us.

Mariella learned about finances with her husband, and through their marriage in partnership, he taught her about dealing with taxes, her savings, CDs, and banks. He also taught her how to protect their financial future.

This Kaleidoscope Woman does not like taking conventional medicine. She prefers more natural means to good health. It has been about three years since she exercised regularly, but she still walks, swims, and stays active. She is not the type of woman to sit in front of the television and binge watch programs. She always has something to do.

At this point in her life, intimacy is more important than sex itself. After forty-seven years of marriage, it's still there from time to time but after having issues with menopause, she knows intimacy is most important.

Faith is the number one priority for this Kaleidoscope Woman. She believes that without it, you lose yourself, your life, and everything. "Faith is what holds you together and keeps you sane." Mariella is not a religious person who goes to church every week, but she is definitely a spiritual being.

Politics is not this woman's cup of tea. She does pay attention to the political world, and she hears from and learns a great deal from her husband, but she thinks that politicians are going to do what they want regardless. She does exercise her right to vote. Some of her friends have opposing political views from her own; they keep their friendships by not discussing politics.

Being street smart is just as important as earning a degree. You need the dirty work to be wise and sharpen up and the degree to present yourself.

Mariella received an associate's degree at Miami Dade College and a bachelor's degree in apparel engineering from Florida International University. While working at the Art Institute she began her master's degree but didn't complete it. She started her own company called The Little Gems when she left the Art Institute and worked with retailers and staff to build her label. Since the birth of her grandson, the company has become more like a hobby, but in time, Mariella will continue building the label when she can work at her own pace.

To the little girl within, she says, "Stay focused and follow your passion and dreams, but stay grounded. I have learned about the power of women working together. I will learn to delegate more to my fellow women friends and tell myself, 'Together we win!'"

C H R I S

Real Estate Broker

A CHILD OF THE KING

This Mosaic Man, Chris, is a very spiritual individual. He is honest, caring, loving, trustworthy, and lives with integrity. He is originally from the Bronx, New York, where he lived for twenty-one years before moving to Florida. Chris's inspirations come from God. He loves most music but tends to lean toward more mellow, calming music; usually 93.1 on his radio dial. He always has the radio playing whether in his car or in the barbershop.

Chris loves to play golf and spends a great deal of time studying allegories in the Bible and spiritual interpretation of the Bible that are not being taught in the mainstream churches. He was raised a Catholic, but in his search for true faith, he became a born-again Christian, then a Christian Science follower. After studying all these different faiths, he came to the conclusion that there is no "religion" in God.

Blue, Chris's favorite color, is the color of his eyes. He likes that the color matches his eyes. He is not fond of heights and is claustrophobic. No tight places for him!

People who are caring, loving, and giving are the types of people Chris feels comfortable with in his life. He usually gravitates to the underdog or those no one else would hang out with. He prefers one-on-one friendships and is not comfortable in crowds.

This Mosaic Man enjoys watching *A Bronx Tale, Forrest Gump,* and *Shawshank Redemption*s.

Chris's relationship with his father is just so-so. His father was an alcoholic who became a born again Christian and passed judgment on many of Chris's choices in life. No question, his Dad has been a bigot. Simply put, Chris's dad is a Republican and Chris is a Democrat.

Many of Chris's close friends are spiritual in nature. Surprisingly, they are twenty or thirty years older than he is. He feels he is definitely an old soul.

Faith is Chris's number one priority, even before family or friends. He believes we are "a spiritual being having a human experience." This man believes there is no religion in God, that Oneness will pull us all together and that religion is manmade. We will realize we are one spirit and one God—Omnipotent, Omnipresent, Omnipotent.

Chris is not a gym rat but definitely tries to take care of himself. He works out at home by doing push-ups, sit-ups, and jumping jacks at least three times a week. He takes vitamins but doesn't like doctors. He tries to solve his health issues by himself through meditation. The words "meditation" and "medication" both mean to heal. There was a time before Chris found his faith in God that he did not like what he saw in the mirror and thought about leaving the planet. He was miserable and didn't want to be here. He didn't know anything about mind, body, and spirit. He didn't know about God and wanted to "check out." One night he had a massive headache and said to God, "If you're real, heal this headache right now!" He sat up in bed and the headache was gone. He lay in bed and wept. It has become apparent to Chris that in order to be successful, you have to love yourself.

Sex is loved and needed by this Mosaic Man. He thinks it's great and helps deal with stress. It is a beautiful thing to share between two people. It's the passion and healing for the mind, body, and spirit. Chris was very insecure as a young man and went through many relationships before meeting his present girlfriend, who he cares very much for. In the past, he always ended the relationships first before the girls could leave him.

"If God is an infinite supplier, why would his child lack anything?" When this Mosaic Man believed that finances would come but the mental part had to come first, the river and flow came. Chris found a $10,000 bracelet and prayed he would find the owner; he did and she was ever so grateful. At that moment, God said to him that he would never be lacking in finances, and he hasn't been.

After high school, Chris studied hotel management but after a year, he was unhappy with his field of study and switched to a two-year degree in criminal justice.

Politics is not an area of interest for Chris. He hasn't thought it through yet, but thinks perhaps there should be no party lines—only the House and Senate. This man has gotten a few speeding tickets in his life, but they were given while driving by himself.

This Mosaic Man began buzzing his head in high school and graduated to buzzing his friends' heads. He never thought he would do it for a living. Since he was a kid, he had worked in a delicatessen in his neighborhood and thought he would become a chef but eventually switched to criminal justice. In 1994 he moved to Florida from New York. He worked a short time in a hair salon but was not happy there and left.

Chris felt the Holy Spirit led him into the real estate business for fifteen years, but in 2006–2008, the market fell apart and he started his own transportation company. He advertised in the same place he ran his real estate ads.

LOVE IS God!

To the little boy within, Chris says, "Don't be scared. God is with you and holding your hand. There is nothing to fear, and love yourself, you schmuck! You are wonderful and beautiful and a child of the King!"

DR. SF

Psychiatrist

FEELING GOOD

Dr. SF is very slow to anger and at times can be shy but is open and very interested in learning new things. This Mosaic Man is adventurous and enjoys improving the world and people's lives.

Family is the inspiration for Dr. SF. He believes that he is on this earth for a purpose and is interested in contributing to the sense of direction for human civilization. Because he is a physician, at times he wonders if he himself has possible illnesses, but whatever ails him usually turn out to be minor.

While Dr. SF is open to meeting new people, he is particular about who he lets close to him, especially who he trusts. He is not quick to establish meaningful relationships.

Snorkeling, hitting the beach, and backpacking are a few of This Mosaic Man's hobbies. He also enjoys travel and all types of music and is an abstract oil painter and guitarist.

LOVE IS universal!

Family is the number one priority for Dr. SF. Their well-being comes before anything else. He is married with a step-daughter and is very close with his family in Florida and his parents in the Midwest.

This Mosaic Man does not transcribe to any specific religion. He believes we are in the universe to serve a spiritual purpose.

Dr. SF tries not to be hypocritical when it comes to health. As a physician, sometimes he faces distractions, but he makes an effort to eat healthily, sleep well, and maintain a balance between health and work. Deepening the connection with his wife is Dr. SF's approach to sexuality.

He still has more to learn about financial management, but his parents were always fiscally responsible. He is not miserly but tries not to put himself into precarious positions.

Sunshine of the Spotless Mind is one of Dr. SF's favorite movies. Soccer is his favorite sport, but he played basketball because of his height.

Dr. SF believes there is a big difference between the wisdom of day-to-day life situations and formal education. His parents always emphasized a formal education as a top priority because it allows educational pursuits and creates greater opportunities. Dr. SF's dad was a professor at a business school, so, by default, Dr. SF's undergraduate work was in economics. Fortunately, that didn't capture his attention, and in his sophomore year studied the function of the human brain and the relationship between the brain and psychological experiences; that area of medicine grabbed his attention.

To the little boy within, Dr. SF says, "Don't be afraid to pursue your dream and have high ambitions!"

CHAPTER TWENTY FIVE

LOURDES

Retired Flight Attendant

THE WILDFLOWER

Lourdes absolutely identifies with the Kaleidoscope Woman; in fact she calls herself a bohemian cultural creative. Such a person is concerned with the environment, nature, music, art, and theater. She considers herself to be a woman with a warrior's heart and a fighting spirit. She is also extremely inquisitive, an independent thinker, and a free spirit. Lourdes tries to live by six pillars of life: explore, learn, grow, create, share, celebrate.

Fear of heights is the only phobia this woman faces. She has often been asked, "If you are afraid of heights, why are you a flight attendant?" As long as she was enclosed in a cabin, she was fine. It's when she's standing on the top of a mountain or at a roof party in New York that she must stand away from the edge.

Cobalt blue is the aura and color of this Kaleidoscope Woman. Each zodiac sign has a color aura, and Lourdes is a Sagittarian—a fire sign whose color is blue. Mediterranean blue and azure blue are also her colors because they are calming.

Music, art, Gregorian chants, blues, Latin music, and drums move this Kaleidoscope Woman. She is a spiritual being and is inspired by meditation; getting into the flow of being, being in the now, making time stop all affect her spirit.

Her mother's father gave Lourdes the spark to entertain. He was a devoted partner and sang opera. He used to teach Lourdes to sing folk songs, and he also taught her to write and read poetry. He nurtured the flame for creativity. Her grandmother, who used to read the Bible and discuss all the saints, inspired Lourdes's spiritual side. Lourdes also gained her writing skills from her grandmother.

Family is number one to this Kaleidoscope Woman. She is very close with her mother although they have "butted heads" in the past. She loves her mother fiercely but realizes they are totally different women. Her mother is conventional and wanted Lourdes to be a certain way. Her mother was also closer with her baby sister—who followed their mother around dotingly—than with Lourdes. After the passing of her sister, Lourdes and her mother have come to terms with each other.

Lourdes and her older son have intuitiveness running between them. Her middle son is married, and, unfortunately, she doesn't get along with her daughter-in-law. The middle child is stuck in "middle child syndrome," where the eldest and youngest of the family received the most attention for different reasons and he's still in the middle. Lourdes and her daughter have the most in common. Her daughter is a singer, dancer, and actress. They can brainstorm together. Her cousins were her best friends. As a note of interest, Lourdes was the closest with members of the family who are no longer living. She doesn't have many close female friends.

This Kaleidoscope woman considers herself to be an assertive woman, and finds that sometimes people don't know how to deal with that. Lourdes is uninhibited and has a secondary family of people who mentor her—for example, her flamenco teacher who she shared a very close connection with. It went beyond dancing and was very spiritual. With any relationship, Lourdes needs a connection on a spiritual level.

Faith is the only thing that keeps this Kaleidoscope Woman going. She has felt a deep spirituality since she was very young. As a child, Lourdes used to have imaginary friends. From the age of three until sixteen, she dreamt about her grandmother as an angel coming to visit her. After age sixteen, the dreams stopped.

Taking care herself is very important to Lourdes. Eat healthy and stay active is her motto. She deals with hypothyroid medication but otherwise is in good shape.

Lourdes's relationship with finances is a spotty one. She invested in apartments in Spain, but when the market crashed in 2008, she felt the loss. That was something beyond her control. Trial and error is how she has learned about money. She could have stayed married and comfortable but decided to simplify her home. She went from a five-bedroom house to a two-bedroom condominium.

Although she didn't finish her college studies, education is very important to this Kaleidoscope Woman. She's gained much of her education through reading and traveling. As a flight attendant, Lourdes learned the history and geography of many countries. She became street smart by living in New York. She is comfortable traveling alone and enjoys it.

"Learning to be comfortable in your own skin" is key to enjoying sex, Lourdes says. She's comfortable with pleasing herself and must feel a connection with a person before sleeping with them.

Born and raised in San Francisco, this woman is politically very liberal. She is definitely progressive in politics. Having traveled and lived with foreign flight attendants, she considers herself an international woman.Lourdes is a first generation Nicaraguan American, so Spanish is her mother tongue. While traveling the world, she never felt American; she was more a "citizen of the world."

Lourdes worked for many years as a flight attendant with United and Eastern Airlines. Her neighborhood consisted of international people, including Chinese and Nicaraguan recent immigrants, and Lourdes knew already at ten years old that she wanted to see the world.

LOVE IS eternal.

CHAPTER TWENTY-SIX

AIMEE

Teacher

PROUD MAMA BEAR

Aimee definitely identifies with being a Kaleidoscope Woman. She has many layers and considers herself to be strong, loving, and very passionate in everything she does. She is loyal and generous and tries to instill much of these qualities into her son, who is number one in her life.

Bright pink is the aura of this Kaleidoscope woman because she considers herself to be very feminine. It's a strong pink, a powerful and electric pink!

This woman is inspired by people who are down-to-earth, authentic, and kind. Those people find a space in her life. It is important that the people who share her life see the best in everyone, including her. Of course, her son and husband are a big inspiration to her every day.

Aimee's husband and son are her top priority in life. It's important to her that she make time to be involved in family life.

Friendships are important to this Kaleidoscope woman, and they also play an important role in the raising of her son. Friendships can be family.

Aimee's family is interfaith family, so it's important to her that her son learns both his mother's and father's faith—Christian and Jewish, respectively.

Aimee is a healthy woman. She thinks some people take their health for granted and complain over nothing when they shouldn't. She believes it's important to stay as active and healthy as possible.

Intimacy in marriage is very important to Aimee. She believes in taking the time with her spouse to make intimacy a priority, because it is a very important part of keeping the relationship alive.

Aimee and her husband both handle their finances; it's a 50/50 partnership. This woman learned about finances in high school when she opened bank accounts and began understanding budgets. She is pleased to see personal finance literacy being taught in school today.

"Very, very, very important!" is how this Kaleidoscope Woman views education. It was a priority in her life and her that of her husband, and she will make it a priority for her son as well. She holds the very highest standards for education. She and her husband continue to take professional development classes and will set high standards for her son.

Staying neutral is Aimee's political approach in life. She tries not to get too wrapped up into the day-to-day of politics and is not involved directly in order to avoid being overwhelmed by today's politics.

LOVE IS authentic!

"Do what you love, and you will never work a day in your life," is Aimee's philosophy about work. She is proud to be a teacher and hopes she is a role model by leading the way for future high school students. Aimee has been successful in the professional fields of teaching, business, and fashion.

To the little girl within, Aimee says, "Stay the course, stay inspired, and be true to you. Keep smiling!"

M E R Y L

Certified Akashic Consultant
Certified Energy Healer

A DIFFERENT PERSPECTIVE

Much of what is revealed by Meryl are concepts.

Meryl definitely identifies with the Kaleidoscope Woman. She is funny, fun, serious when she needs to be, thoughtful, and kind with an inner strength. She is perseverant and has the ability to help people feel better—a healer, humble, modest, and not yet one hundred percent ambitious. She has an adventurous side and is fearless in facing life.

Meryl's aura is dependent upon how she is feeling. She feels a healing power with color. It affects what she decides to wear and eat. Color is a frequency, and translucent white is the color she identifies with since it encompasses all color.

The magic of how different every day can be is what inspires and motivates Meryl—the surprises around the corner . . . Love! A connection to everything inspires her to be the best she can be to remain connected and shine to the collective.

The people in Meryl's life are uplifting, inspiring, positive people like herself. Yet, at the same time, they represent a variety of personalities. Meryl believes that we all learn from each other. She is careful who she lets 100 percent into her life; she has to feel them out first. Not everyone can join the Meryl club. She is selective because of her awareness.

Meryl believes people and family come into one's life for a reason. She believes that her soul needs lessons and that it chooses families for specific karmic reasons that will be revealed for higher clearing and bliss. At this time, she has a good relationship with her family. In the past, it was tumultuous.

Friends are a joy to Meryl, and that is how she relates to them— with Joy. With them, ideas flow about how to have fun and help society.

Faith, for Meryl, is based on spirituality rather than religion. Everything is based on spirituality—work, thoughts, and actions. Spirituality is her joy and lights up her heart.

This Kaleidoscope Woman feels GREAT! She doesn't visit doctors and feels healthy and wonderful while going through her post-menopausal stage of her life.

Sex plays an important role is her life, and Meryl believes you can always use more! More is more!!

Meryl's relationship with money is changing. It used to be carefree. Now it's a spiritual thing. Money is a means for survival and fun, and in the present moment it's OK for what it is. There is no future and past. Her thought are evolving on money.

This Kaleidoscope Woman is well educated and asks, "What is education? To Meryl, the important education is the spiritual one;

spiritual classes regarding healing and other classes and experiences that propelled her and excited her.

Regarding politics/law, Meryl believes that what we are experiencing now is necessary. She feels that for the evolution of humanity, we need to experience the full darkness to understand it, release it, and embrace the full light of who we truly are. She feels that what is happening is all an illusion. It is the illusion of duality and separateness. So, if we are love, then it stands to reason that we have to love everything that is happening. And if that's the case, then she has to help others do that as well. She fully believes that light and justice will prevail and that we will all move in the light because we are all one . . . one love baby!

Meryl is a professional and works at it. She finds it funny to say this because some people have a hard time separating who they are from what they do. She is a certified Healer and Reiki Master. She is also a certified Practitioner of Magnified Healing™, Phase I and III. She is a Light Source Practitioner and Akashic Records certified Teacher and Consultant.

Meryl's message to fellow Kaleidoscope Women is to shine your light, bring your mission to fruition, be your authentic self with joy, and be kind to one another in this time of evolution for humanity and the woman.

To the little girl within, Meryl says, "Do your thing, listen to your gut. I love you, support you, and will never leave you. Be yourself, because who you are is pretty great! Be slow to anger and quick to love."

CHAPTER TWENTY-EIGHT

LISA G

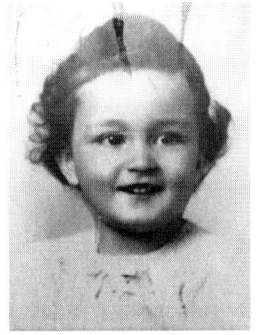

Retired Business Woman

DON'T GIVE UP OR GIVE IN

Yes! Lisa absolutely identifies with the Kaleidoscope Woman, and she reacts to the people around her in a variety of ways. If she is speaking with men, she talks stocks. If she is speaking with women, she talks about babies and cooking. Her interactions fluctuate because she is gay. Lisa has always hidden behind titles. She is honest, loving, a writer, and a mother to many children who call her "Ma." She is also a nurturing and loving daughter.

Purple is the aura and essence of this Kaleidoscope Woman, along with tones of brown. Purple reflects spring, and brown reflects the sketches she has drawn as well as pictures she has taken. She hates black and white.

Lisa is moved by someone who speaks well and is educated; that inspires her to sit up straight and meet them at their level.

The people in this woman's life are kind and willing to be flexible. They are not moody and do not curse—she hates cursing. These people are kind and thoughtful with depth to them.

When this Kaleidoscope Woman was a little girl, she wanted to be a little boy. Between the ages of three and five, she carried a boy's wallet with an ID named Joe, who was an elevator operator. Of course, all this was made up. When she was about five, her mother pushed her into frilly dresses. Lisa felt her parents played her like a tennis ball; if she talked with her mother, her father was angry. If she talked with her father; her mother got angry. It was always a tennis match.

To Lisa, family is NOT number one. Friends are number one. Family is exhausting! You always have to cater to family. In a way, she worries about what her family will do with her as she ages. But "friends will always protect me," she says.

For Lisa, friends hold the number one spot, but lovers hold history. She is very bitter about her father, who was nasty and cold. Both she and her brother feared him. Her brother stuttered because of his fear, and Lisa was constantly frightened.

This Kaleidoscope Woman leans on her religion and faith very much. It gives her strength, yet she is still doubtful about whether the Bible is the truth. She knows it's a book, but how truthful is it and who wrote it? It gives her comfort to think of an afterlife for all of the people she's loved who are now gone.

Health . . . what about it?? Lisa has been fighting health issues since she was twenty-four and is now in her seventies. Once, she had to learn to walk all over again and then dealt with different illnesses: cancer, diabetes, a heart condition, and a broken heart. She has often told doctors that they have more photos of her than her momma does. OH . . . and Parkinson's disease. "I try to avoid it. It's a diminishing disease that can't be cured, and the ultimate end is the end. I omit it from my thoughts daily." Every morning she gets up is a challenge. She can't stand or move, which is awful. But she pushes through it. She is a very strong woman.

Knowing she is a lesbian would probably turn off a number of people. She has experienced people back up and not hug her when they found out, or pull their children away for fear she might cuddle them. Or some have refused to kiss her. She has always hidden her true self.

Her relationship with money is not good. This Kaleidoscope Woman takes too many gambles, although she feels she is getting too old to be going into debt. Sometimes she is careless and not frugal, and then she is shocked to wake up and see that her checkbook doesn't balance. She's still trying to get out of debt.

Education is most important to her, but superior to college education is the school of common sense. Without common sense, you can't have a peaceful life. "Close the book and learn about life by living it!"

Lisa holds a high respect for the law. She has never gotten a traffic ticket. Politics are important and are how our country runs. She always votes in presidential elections; sometimes she's happy with the results and sometimes miserable, but doesn't let the outcomes run her life.

Sex for this Kaleidoscope Woman is at the bottom of her bucket list. At this point in her life, friendship is more important. She prefers women because of their beauty, scent, and gracious loveliness. Toys - Eh, good in a pinch, but not as a daily diet.

Lisa Gaye is a retired business woman, author, artist, photographer, and inventor. She enjoys working in creative fields. She was involved in advertising and owned a business for ten years. The food industry took her from poverty to East Hampton, and East Hampton took her to a comfortable future!

LOVE IS a profound experience.

To the little girl within, Lisa G. says, "Be yourself and don't hide over the years, like I did!"

J E N N I F E R

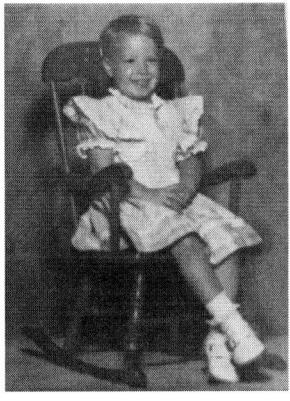

Cancer Genetic Counselor

EMBRACE THE EVOLUTION

There are two Kaleidoscope Women in Jennifer's life. First, Jennifer identifies with the KW woman, and then there is her mom. Jen's impression of her mom has changed with age, as she's watched her mom grow and change and go through so many difficult experiences. While Jen didn't notice it until she was older, she now sees that her mom gives selflessly to other people and that her strength to deal with her son's mental illness is impressive.

Jen's woman is also selfless and giving, and her ability to see more than one issue makes her open-minded. Until recently, she didn't realize how strong she was.

Her mother's aura is orange, because she is warm and caring. Jen's aura changes from bright pink, when she feels positive, to blue when her mood saddens.

Her mom is inspired by kindness, and Jen is inspired by helping her family and patients. She is a cancer genetic counselor and enjoys helping her patients, kids, coworkers, and family feel safe and loved.

Jen's mom is a life saver for her, keeping her grounded and afloat. Jen is excited about the fact that, like a Kaleidoscope, she has the power to change the view, surroundings, and perception of her life.

This Kaleidoscope woman relates to her family as the control center, helping to captain the ship; she is in charge of multiple things and makes sure they get done.

Jen's relationship with her friends is a two-way street; they help her, and she, in turn, helps support them with kindness, love, and friendship.

Faith plays a big role in Jen's life; it provides strength and encouragement. It also allows her to continue with life and try new views.

Unfortunately, health does not always take a priority in Jen's life. It takes balancing it in your life and also needs to play an important role in your life.

Sex sometimes takes a lower part in Jen's life, and, like the Kaleidoscope, the priority of the pieces shift, making the view more beautiful.

Finances? Simple - They are a stressful necessity.

Education enriches every part of Jen's life. Her master's degree in genetic counseling allows her to be a cancer specialist and help educate and empower individuals to make choices about genetic testing for inherited cancer risk. She loves the job, and the sixteen years she has devoted so far to her patients. Her profession certainly gives her a perspective on life, but it can also be emotionally exhausting.

Jen's mom, at sixty-seven, is very politically active, especially since Jen left for college. Jen is aware of political events, but not generally invested in them. She felt badly, however, when families were being separated at the border.

Jen is raising her daughters to be strong and respectful; she tries to create an environment of freedom for them as well as teach them to respect the freedom of others. She encourages the girls to form their own opinions on issues.

She believes that, like a Kaleidoscope, there are many facets to love—love of soulmate, family, friends, and colors. After her divorces, new images of her life were created and she is facing the changes with strength and grace.

To the little girl within, Jennifer says, "Always keep your chin up and embrace who you are. There is always a better version of you just around the bend!"

CHAPTER THIRTY

RICHARD D

Retired Graphic Designer

SAILING THROUGH LIFE

Richard is most definitely a spiritual man—a Christian. His mom first took him to Christian spiritual reunions when he was five. At an early age, Richard experienced reincarnation, and then saw the future on occasion. He has also seen the past, present, and future cosmic consciousness.

One sister is all the family this Mosaic Man has left today. Richard was with his mom when she passed away. Unfortunately, Richard's wife passed away about four years ago. Richard had been married to his wife for twenty-three years, and had actually known her for almost fifty years. She was his true love. He found her by running into her daughter at a train station many years after first meeting her. He recognized the daughter and asked for her mother's telephone number, and, as they say, the rest is history.

Good souls and people who are givers, not takers, are the ones Richard lets into his life. It's a plus if they are spiritual and religious.

This man takes good care of himself, although he's not a gym rat. He remembers his great-grandmother sitting in a rocking chair smoking a cigar, and she lived a long time (smile). Richard is a vegetarian for spiritual reasons. "As long as it's not running around before you eat it, it's OK," he says.

Richard's approach to sexuality is, "As we age, the sex slows down." Richard is a little old-fashioned and is not happy unless his partner is happy.

Richard still hasn't learned about finances! BUT . . . he's good with working with what he has and lives within his means. As a child, he wasn't given an allowance and was taught that whatever money he earned while working under the family roof went to the family. SO . . . he stopped working (smile).

This Mosaic Man went to a Maritime high school where half a day of classes was held on a Liberty Ship. At the age of seventeen, he went to sea in the Merchant Marines. He sailed on and off for about eight years.

When Richard was sixteen years old, he learned to play the congas and he met a friend at the Maritime Union Hall who played the saxophone and had studied at Julliard School of Music. The two of them decided to put together a five-piece Latin band. Another friend who played with the group Blues Magoos said they were looking for a conga player and invited Richard to play on one of their albums.

Inspired by his first wife, Richard decided to attend Hunter College. He originally went for physical therapy, but after not doing well in the biology and organic chemistry courses, he changed directions and studied commercial art graphics. After one semester, he got his first art job but left after two weeks for the Merchant Marines for the last time.

When he returned from sea, Richard worked as a graphic commercial artist for companies like Avon, Holt, Reinhart and Winston, and Publishers Clearing House.

Yes, Richard is politically active. He votes regularly and is a member of the National Committee to preserve Social Security and Medicare. He sends petitions regularly to senators and congressmen regarding social security. He has never been ticketed for his driving, though he does admit to speeding. Just not getting caught (smile).

LOVE IS giving without wanting anything in return.

Motorcycle riding, sailing, and dabbling in computer graphics are some of Richard's hobbies.

To the little boy within, Richard says, "Believe in God, and be open to God!"

CHAPTER THIRTY-ONE

CHERYL

Operations Administrator

SEXY GRANDMA

Cheryl is in her sixties and definitely identifies with The Kaleidoscope Woman. She is full of life and ideas, happy and colorful. Whether she is out in the world alone or not, in her sixties she wants to live life, work hard, and live her golden years traveling and learning about new things and meeting new people.

Cheryl is funny and cute and enjoys learning about other people. She is full of love and loves romance, and does not like bullying, hate, or mean people. She definitely fights for her principles.

Pink is the color of her aura because it's pretty and springy. She is inspired by life, getting out of bed every day, dancing, and happiness. She lives a peaceful life.

LOVE IS a beautiful thing.

Family, friends, and coworkers are inspired by this Kaleidoscope Woman. She allows kind, happy, honest, good, thoughtful, and positive people in her life. No negativity. This woman is excited by never knowing what she's going to do next . . . her funny ways.

A part of this woman is affected by everyday living. Her message is to live the day to the fullest because tomorrow is promised to no one.

Her family is loving. Although they are scattered, they are always there for one another. She loves her friends and loves being with them. She has a strong belief in God and in health and taking care of yourself. She says to take care of yourself because if you don't, no one else will. Drink lots of water, exercise, do prescreening checkups—pap smear, mammogram, and colonoscopy.

Money can't buy love, but you need money to survive. Cheryl's a hard worker and wants to earn money on her own. She believes college is necessary nowadays, because companies look for degrees but sometimes miss the common sense in people.

Better than just sex, companionship plays an important role in Cheryl's life as she gets older. As we know, the body changes with age and doesn't work the way it used to. She believes in abortion in the first trimester but not in late term abortions.

She doesn't enjoy talking about politics because, whether with friends or family, it usually ends up in a fight. Cheryl avoids politics, but she does believe that women deserve equal pay if not more, because some women do a better job in their work than men.

This Kaleidoscope Woman is inspired by all kinds of love: for children, family, soulmate. Sometimes you fall in love, and then as you get older, things change. What was once important at forty is not as important at sixty.

Two thoughts from Cheryl: Not my circus, not my monkey! Live for today, tomorrow is not promised!

To the little girl within, Cheryl says, "Never stop believing in yourself, and never give up!"

S A D E

Optometry Technician

CELESTIAL INTENTIONS

Absolutely, Sade is a Kaleidoscope Woman: strong, courageous, fearless, and a Proverbs 31 woman. She is a special kind of spiritual woman who serves others and would like to control her environment, whether at work or home. She keeps her eyes off of herself by giving to others and has learned that through vulnerability you find strength.

Sade has learned to be intentional about friendships. She spent a few years partaking in reckless behavior but now has many friends with similar value systems, who she has chosen intentionally. Sade appreciates good friends. There was time when she didn't understand true, loyal friendship. She happened to have met her special mentor through friends; through their connection, Sade learned that she does not have to compromise who is in a relationship. This became an open door to being authentic and willing to help others. Her mentor is in her thirties and has opened doors to meeting amazing women.

Faith is Sade's first priority, and family is her second. Grandma, who was a Jehovah's Witness, raised this Kaleidoscope Woman. Sade came from a broken home because neither parent was available to raise the seven children in her family. Feeling so alone, Sade thought about suicide and attempted to drown herself. But she felt a hand drag her out and knew it was Godwho saved her. She got up and started listening to gospel music. Eventually, Sade came to the states from Jamaica to live with her mother. Since then, her faith has grown, and she knows God had his hand on her.

Very conscientious of being in good health, Sade gives fitness a place of top importance in her life. She enjoys exercising because it represents self-love. In a workout, she is able to be still and focus about her job or her business. It is "a way of life that gives you energy to focus on God's work."

This Kaleidoscope Woman began her sexual journey when she was eighteen years old. She still talks with her first partner but knew that with that person she hadn't searched for "God's desire for your heart." After trying a relationship with a second partner, Sade knew that being celibate was the path for her. She is now committed to waiting for her husband and thinks abundance, not scarcity, is the answer, as well as patience.

No one modeled financial management for Sade as she was growing up. Her mentor has helped her learn to budget. Now Sadie tells money where to go instead of money telling her where to go.

Sade dropped out of college in Tallahassee where she studied psychology. She believes that times are changing and that true knowledge can also come from life experiences. Sade loves helping people, but there were too many limits in psychology. She looks forward to the point in her life where she can make a global impact and believes it can be done through personal growth—learning from people who have been on the path of success.

Politics is very basic to this Kaleidoscope Woman: "I'm a big advocate for the free enterprise system." And no, she's never gotten a speeding ticket.

Purple is Sade's favorite color because it represents royalty.

This Kaleidoscope Woman's first job was in the retail clothing industry. She was assistant manager when she met her mentor and was later recruited into the optometry field. Leaving her first position because it was a "dog-eat-dog" environment, her mentor asked her one day, "How do you want to live your life?" Sade replied, "I want a life of abundance, where I am debt-free and can serve people in Jamaica and abroad, and change my family tree and live a free woman! God's gift to you is life, and your gift to him is what you do with it!" Another word of advice from her mentor was to find someone who lives the life you want to live and convince them to coach and mentor you.

"The Dream" is what inspires and moves this woman. She used to be moved by adversity and pushed to overcome it. Now she knows what's available and she is fired up about the dream.

Do not show lizards or insects to Sade. But worse than that is her only true fear—that five years from now she will be in the same position she's currently in.

Hobbies are a fun sport for Sade. She loves "dream building." She will visit million-dollar properties and sit in expensive sports cars; everything to make the dream real. She loves music, the spoken word, poetry, and water by the beach because it brings clarity.

LOVE IS kind and patient.

The Pursuit of Happiness and *Daddy's Little Girl* are a few of her favorite movies.

To the little girl within, Sade says, "Don't allow people's opinions to hinder you from becoming the woman you aspire to be. Be authentic!"

CHAPTER THIRTY-THREE

WILLIAM

Professional Musician

NOTES TO FOREVER

William considers himself to be sincere, down to earth, and giving, but these qualities have been his downfall. He is strong and extremely loyal. Black is his go-to color because it is strong and goes with everything.

A beautiful woman who is kind and giving moves this man. When he was about nine years old, he heard The Beatles and fell in love with their music.

This Mosaic Man will let people who are sincere into his life. When he allowed questionable people into his life in the past, he got burned by them. He has learned from his mistakes, and it has made him a stronger individual.

LOVE IS great!

A WOMAN IS beautiful!

Family is number one for William. Always has been and always will be. William has good relationships with his family, though he has been "fucked over a few times" by them. He has been married once but has no children. He does regret not creating his own family. He was told he has a son in Minnesota and pursued the lead to no end. Family is everything!

William describes his social life as "a handful of friends but hundreds of acquaintances." When he does make a friend, they are special and last a lifetime. One friend in particular is like a brother; they even have the same last name.

In lieu of playing guitar on the stages of the world, William now plays in his church for God. When he was a kid, his mom didn't want him to play rock n' roll, but a friend taught him to play guitar, and he's been playing ever since.

About twelve years ago, this Mosaic Man suffered a brain hemorrhage. It took almost two years to recover. Today, he is doing well.

William feels he should have finished his four-year college degree. He does have two years of majoring in English. Street smarts have helped in his success. The band Sugarcane was a stepping stone to building his musical career. Rima, the female lead in his group, sang in such difficult song keys that she helped William to learn transposing. This Mosaic Man is a self-taught musician.

"I love sex!" William says. But he has learned throughout years of being with different women on the road that it's always nice to have the right partner. "It's a privilege" if you find a friend and lover, he says. Unfortunately, William's marriage ended when his touring schedule started affecting it. Though he tried to live a more stable life with the in-laws, the lack of privacy took its toll on the marriage and his wife felt it was her turn.to find happiness.

This Mosaic Man was raised a Republican even though he always liked the Democrats. Today, he is an Independent and votes according to issues.

Being buried alive and scared of the dark are William's fears and phobia.

This man's favorite movies are *Raging Bull, The Passion of the Christ,* and *Forrest Gump.*

This Mosaic Man has worked in a gas station and a supermarket and has been a driver, waiter, and lead guitarist. He respects people who make an honest living, because he has been there. He knows he won't go for the fast buck if it's offered. He loved playing the clubs and was very shy when he started playing the guitar. He built his confidence with the group Sugarcane.

To the little boy within, William says, "You should have finished school."

CHAPTER THIRTY-FOUR

GINA

CEO/President
Women That Soar

A DIVINE CONNECTION

Gina identifies with the Father-and-daughter Christ relationship. Her earthly father gave her words of wisdom that have helped her today. She goes to her heavenly father with problems and waits for knowledge. She "downloads" the wisdom to carry out the task on this journey. She thinks women were put here to complement one another. There is an order to life and Gina believes she can't change today; so when she is weak, she rests and turns to God.

Gina describes herself as wise, funny, and sees humor in everything. When we laugh more, she believes, we don't distort things, and laughter overcomes more complicated issues. Laughter is the joy in life, and you must laugh in the midst of pain. Gina also considers herself to be strong, faithful, and compassionate. Her friends dubbed her Harriet Tubman because of her ability to let go, let God, and overcome obstacles in front of her.

With great success comes great responsibility is Gina's belief. She understands that achieving success often requires overcoming enormous challenges. She experiences a battle of faith, more than she wants to bear sometimes, but the Lord gives her what she lacks.

White is the color Gina gravitates to because it is pure in nature, but Navy was the color selected for her appearance on the "2019 Women that Soar Awards" on television.

Being able to be of service to other people is what inspires Gina. She also tries to encourage others. If she enlightens, empowers, and encourages then she is living with a purpose. The people Gina lets into her life usually make her laugh, or they conduct deep conversations. They are educated and stimulate her mind.

Family is the number one priority in Gina's life. She loves being with her family and has two daughters and two sons, who mean everything to her. Her mom and dad handed down her morals, principals, and values.

Gina also thinks it's important to have good friends in her life to call on, share with, cry with, and have a solid loyal relationship with. She does not have a multitude of friends, but the ones she does have are loyal and there for her.

Health for Gina involves the mind, body, and spirit. Her philosophy is when you don't feel well, exercise and feed the body. The nourishment of God's word is used to treat the body as a temple.

As a young woman, Gina did not apply her knowledge to money. It wasn't until her thirties that Gina started learning and focusing on finances. She has been married for twenty years, and she and her husband handle the finances together as a team.

Gina believes that love and touch should be incorporated whenever possible in a loving relationship, with the right partner.

Gina believes that formal education is important as well as educating each other daily. What is taught in the classroom is structure. Formal education is a process, and life lessons are not taught in school. They take you through life and give you wisdom, teaching you how to move when you can't see to go left or right.

Gina votes but stays away from the day-to-day of politics. She has only gotten one ticket for speeding in her entire life.

Gina's professional life has brought her to the position today of CEO and president of Women That Soar. She has worked in sports entertainment and public relations but did not feel fulfilled in those jobs. So she asked God to show her and reveal to her how she could be of service. Now she inspires, enlightens, and encourages women from around the world.

LOVE IS unconditional, patient, and long-suffering.

To the little girl within, Gina says, "Don't be afraid. Everything will work out fine."

CHAPTER THIRTY-FIVE

RAY

Professional Ice Skater/Coach

THE BRIGHT SIDE OF LIFE

Ray is the type of man who gets up in the morning and likes to have things to do. He likes to keep moving and doing what he enjoys. He stays away from negative people. As a youngster, he was not very patient, but has developed patience with age. Ray has a great sense of humor, and his strength is finding humor in everything. Don't dwell on the negative, he advises. This Mosaic Man does not enjoy checking his devices all day and would much rather speak by telephone to his friends and family.

There are no phobias to worry about with Ray.

As a child, he learned how important money and finances are. He grew up with the concern about not having enough money to support himself or a family. Since Ray has not married, he has not had to worry about having money for the house, mortgage, marriage, and kids. He didn't like to work at jobs he didn't like because he didn't want to get "stuck" in them. His only fear was he did not know if he would be successful enough to support himself and family.

Everyday life inspires this Mosaic Man. He enjoys every day with a positive attitude and tries to do the same for others. He thinks "music is the heartbeat to the soul!" It's everything.

Ray enjoys the company of creative people; ones who are not moody or full of drama that drags a person down. He has always enjoyed the company of positive people, with no prejudices or hatred toward anyone.

During his free time, Ray rides his motorcycle or checks out vintage cars. He would even say that eating healthy is a hobby because he reads and studies up on the effects of food on the human body.

Some of his favorite movies are *My Cousin Vinny*, *The Bronx Tale*—because it reminds him of his upbringing—and the classic musicals with Fred Astaire or Gene Kelly.

Good family relationships are number one to Ray. His dad died when he was seven, and though the extended family had money, his mom decided to raise the children alone. He learned at an early age not to "blow" money. Money gives you the freedom to live life the way you want. His cousins had rich, fancy cars and houses, but Ray never cared for those things; he wanted the security of money for his freedom.

After working in a butcher shop and being taken to a slaughter house, Ray decided to become a vegetarian for two reasons: 1) for health reasons, which he studied a great deal about and 2) because he believes killing the animals is a no-no.

Though raised a Catholic, this Mosaic Man doesn't have a specific philosophy nor is he connected to any organized religion. He lives by the Ten Commandments and believes if you follow them and do the right thing, you don't have to worry about what happens to your soul.

LOVE IS trying to bring happiness to other people.

This Mosaic Man is not very involved in politics. He is neither a Democrat nor Republican. He always votes on issues and not by party. He is concerned that the present party is destroying our country.

Ray studied business and pre-med in college, but he didn't graduate. His life was teaching him that in order to survive life, he had to have street smarts as well. In addition, show business was catching his attention. Ray lived in Little Italy in New York until the age of eight, then to Brooklyn and then to Jackson Heights, Queens. While he was hanging with the street gangs, the Police Athletic League offered the kids sports, one of which was hockey. Ray enjoyed the sport, but his mom thought it would be nice if he learned to skate, so she arranged for lessons. That was it for Ray; he really enjoyed the creative ice skating and music. It was more appealing than the other sports, and that's where the girls were. Ice skating appealed to Ray as a sport and an art form. He enjoyed "selling" the music to the audience, and he had to work hard to be successful, but he enjoyed it enough to work hard. Ray has performed with professional ice shows throughout the world.

To the little boy within, Ray says, "Follow your dreams. Always be good to other people and treat them the way you want to be treated. Don't give up!"

DR. S

Licensed Clinical Psychologist

THIS KALEIDOSCOPE WOMAN POEM

You come to me as I scramble through my daily life and gently remind me that there is peace in slowing down and breathing deeply, in simply noticing the impermanence of life.

You rescue me by showing me how to know myself and remember that as long as I am at home in my heart, I will never be lost.

You nudge me when I see a young child laughing and living or a mother duck leading her ducklings and show my wise mind that knows we are already whole. We are perfect.

You shine your light when gentleness is needed instead of scorn, and urge discernment in conflict. You allow quiet grief when I place my parents in their graves but also tremendous strength to go forward in love.

You provide me with grace when I lose and courage to try again.

Your presence envelops me when I create balance among my professional life, my family, my needs, and my God. Your insistence to know this force I call God constantly burns through my veins until the bigger picture is obvious.

You endure. You love fiercely. You forgive. You wisely choose. You consistently grow.

You are in my laughter and tears, in my words and silence, in my triumphs and silences, in my love and my grief.

With you, I know God. With you, I am complete.